UNDIAGNOSED TO DEATH

How My Mother's Writing Captured Our Family's Hidden Battle with Huntington's Disease

AUDREY ROBERTS
WITH DARLENE GAYNOR

Undiagnosed to Death

How My Mother's Writing Captured Our Family's Hidden Battle
with Huntington's Disease

undiagnosedtodeath.com

Cover Illustration by Darlene Gaynor
Book Design by Transcendent Publishing | TranscendentPublishing.com
Edited by Clare Fernández | TheFireWithinCreative.com

ISBN: 979-8-9992030-2-1

Printed in the United States of America.

CONTENTS

For friends, family, and friends who have become family.

My mother had many, and because of you, she was never alone.

FOREWORD

If you're not familiar with Huntington's disease, one of the key features of the disease is the generational inheritance pattern. If my mom has it, I have a 50% chance of getting it. That's why we talk about autosomal dominance, meaning the gene doesn't skip a generation. It doesn't avoid men or women, and it doesn't affect only the firstborn. You're either born with the gene, or you aren't. These concepts are ingrained in those of us who either live with the disease or treat and care for those who do.

Often referred to by its two-syllable, two-letter moniker, "HD," those familiar with the disease know how the symptoms can impact a patient and their family. Anger, irritability, sleep disturbances, those fidgety movements called chorea, walking challenges, swallowing difficulties, speech slowing, and delusions.

What we don't talk about is the generational trauma that HD brings. Consider a father who starts to get symptoms at 40 years of age and can no longer provide for his family. Maybe his spouse must quit her job to become a full-time caregiver. What happens to that family, to those children? HD will impact those children, and it will also impact the children's children. "To the third and fourth generation …"

Undiagnosed to Death shows us a glimpse of generational trauma and offers us the perspective of one who can describe its taste, smell, and texture. You may not know Audrey, but I have had the opportunity to get to know her this past year. Audrey can talk to you about what it feels like to live through generational trauma. She might tell you about those people in her life who gave her hope or prepared her for university, or what it's like to watch her children grow up as she shares with them the memories of her own childhood.

Audrey has compiled a book that gives us a glimpse into these stories and her journey. I encourage you to read it with an open mind. Let the words and experiences evoke emotions that remind you about life's shared journey with those who have gone before us, but are still with us.

Daniel Claassen, MD, MS
Professor, Neurology,
Vanderbilt University Medical Center
CEO, Huntington's Study Group

INTRODUCTION

M y wedding day was wonderful, but also weighed down by the heavy burden of worrying about my mom. I worried about her arriving on time and whether she was strong enough to even attend the festivities. Things can never be fully about you when you have a family member who is so sick that they need regular care. I was incredibly grateful when my mom's best friend, Stella, wanted to attend the wedding and make a weekend of it. She loved Mom and wanted to enjoy the wedding, of course, but I felt a huge sense of relief knowing that she would also help take care of Mom and make sure she had what she needed.

Still, I spent the whole weekend worried about her. I spent a lot of my young adult years resentful that she couldn't take care of herself. I didn't want to be resentful at my own wedding. This is the weight I carry, replaying every interaction over and over again in my head.

She ended up having a great time at the wedding, even drinking with family at the honky tonks on Broadway, in downtown Nashville, the night before. Looking back, I'm so grateful she was there; I can't imagine what that day would have been like without her.

This is one of my favorite pictures of us together, taken on that day. This was five years before she was diagnosed with

Huntington's disease. The version of her captured in this photo is the one that I want to remember. The Darlene who was full of joy.

I often wonder what life would have been like if I had known much earlier that my mom had a rare genetic disease.

I was raised on a working farm in Tennessee, where I developed an early sense of responsibility and a deep love for community. At just 15 years old, I became the youngest farmers' market manager in my region. That early leadership and desire to contribute were influenced by a quiet truth: I was being raised by a mother who was slowly changing from a disease that no one understood. That mystery and the grace my mother showed through it left an imprint that I continue to carry forward in all that I do.

My mom didn't get the answers she needed in time, and I'm profoundly grateful for the gift of testing negative for Huntington's disease myself. It allows me to tell her story and mine.

Undiagnosed to Death is my way of giving a voice to what was lost and honoring the woman who helped me remember who she was, even as the disease clouded my memories of her.

My path, from growing up on a farm to working in global business, has always been about holding space for others and making sense of things that don't. This memoir is part of that journey. It's a tribute to the mother who quietly carried a rare disease, unknowingly teaching her daughter how to survive with grace, serve with purpose, and remember with clarity.

DIAGNOSIS DAY

I was working at my desk when the phone rang. It was a nurse from Vanderbilt University Medical Center. She said my mother had asked her to call. Mom wanted to schedule a psychiatric evaluation, the first step in being tested for Huntington's disease (HD).

I was used to calls from Mom needing help, but this one felt different. It wasn't one of the usual crises. Those always started with chaos—an incident, a panic. A call about "ramming" shopping carts in the grocery store parking lot. A police officer thinking she was drunk. There had been plenty of those. But this wasn't that. This call felt calm and grounded, yet terrifying in a new way. This was the devil we knew but had been told did not haunt us.

In 2009, ten years earlier, a small-town neurologist told us, "Your mom is as likely to have HD as I am." Meaning very little chance, according to him. Despite her father and brother both having Huntington's, she didn't have tremors like they did. She didn't shake. She was "fine."

But now, this was Vanderbilt. An expert medical team. A proven process. It only took a few questions for me to realize how high her chances really were. My stomach dropped. I felt sick.

My mind started racing, rewinding, fast-forwarding like a film reel spinning out of control. Every crack of my memory lit up with adrenaline. If my mom had HD, that meant there was a

50% chance that I had it, too. That my sister could have it. That our children—my kids and my nieces—were also at risk.

Shit.

I was devastated. Deep down, I'd always known the risk was there, but I had avoided it, whether consciously or unconsciously. The idea of facing a rare, genetic disease often described as the "family killer" was too much to hold. HD mimics Parkinson's, Alzheimer's, and ALS, and symptoms often begin as early as your thirties. I didn't want to believe this could be a possibility for my family.

The nurse at Vanderbilt explained that if Mom passed the psychiatric exam, she would be cleared for genetic testing. If she made it that far, it would be another month before we got the results. I could barely process what she was saying. I couldn't stop thinking about the implications. It wasn't just about my mom anymore. This affected all of us.

Somehow, Mom passed the psych evaluation. It was miraculous, really. They drew her blood, and we waited. A month later, my sister and I went with her to Vanderbilt for her appointment. I remember thinking, *This is the day that could change our entire lives.* When not one but multiple doctors entered the room, that should have been answer enough.

Positive. CAG repeat of 43.

(A CAG repeat is a short sequence of three DNA letters that is repeated many times within the HTT gene, which encodes a protein called huntingtin. Most people without Huntington's disease have fewer than 26 repeats, while having a higher number puts someone at risk of developing the disease or passing it on to their children. In general, the more repeats present, the earlier symptoms may appear.)

"I feel relieved," Mom said quietly.

I felt everything else.

I was thinking about myself. My kids. My sister. My nieces. Every hard moment I'd ever had with my mom, every angry thought, every unkind word. Suddenly, she had an answer for a lifetime of pain and suffering, and I was left with fear and guilt. The counselor in the room gently reminded us that we were still the same people as when we walked in the door. But I didn't feel the same. My whole world had shifted.

Mom and I were always on opposite ends of the spectrum when it came to HD. While I stayed in the dark, detached and unaware, she had become a student of the disease. A frequent visitor to the public library, she researched every symptom, every possibility. She explored dementia, ALS, Alzheimer's—anything that might explain what was happening inside her body. She bought books on brain health and nutrition, but she struggled to implement any changes in her diet. Cooking, eating fresh vegetables, fruits, and lean meats, and following all the healthy recommendations would not only have been expensive but also time-consuming and physically tiring for someone in her health condition. Still, she did her best in other ways. She wrote about her symptoms. She prayed. She turned to faith when she had nothing else to hold. And in the end, Vanderbilt gave her the answer.

It's hard to admit, but in the months following her diagnosis, I realized how much resentment I had been carrying. For years, I watched her change. I watched her lose her spark. But like a parent watching a child grow, the decline was slow, so subtle I couldn't see it clearly. There was so much misunderstanding on my part. Some of it was willful ignorance, some of it hopeful conviction. She hadn't chosen this. She wasn't irresponsible. She was sick. Diagnosis day was a wake-up call. It forced me to reframe everything.

Over time, I watched her fade, piece by piece, from a sharp, creative, joyful soul into someone struggling to survive. It was disheartening and also frustrating. Why couldn't she hold a job? Why couldn't she pay her bills? Why couldn't she simply *care* for herself? I questioned why she acted irrationally. In doing so, I forgot who she was: the woman who dreamed in fabric, who captured light through a camera lens, who saw beauty in every flower.

As she declined, I lost sight of the woman who raised me with faith, hope, and unconditional love. I was too caught up in all the pain. Still, she continued to preach those values, even as her mind slipped away. I had no idea, then, that she would pass less than two years after the HD diagnosis, due to complications from the disease.

And yet, even in illness, she gave. One of the greatest gifts she left was her writing. She wrote most of her life and continued to write until the point when she could no longer do so. She always longed to be a published author. Writing gave her purpose. It was her joy, her outlet, her anchor. Through writing, she found community, healing, and a way to make sense of her world. As I've recovered her writings—family manuscripts, romance novels, poems, songs, essays—I've uncovered memories I thought were gone. She preserved her story, and in doing so, she preserved pieces of all of us.

She wrote under several names. Kathy Knox was her pen name when writing for the local newspaper. She used Gaynor, her maiden name, in other pieces. You'll see those names woven throughout this book, threads in the larger tapestry she began that I am keeping alive.

This story is more than just hers; it's the story of many generations. She wrote a lot about pain and joy, as well as her journey to find healing. She captured her grandparents' stories. And now I'm adding mine. Together, we're completing the work she started and making her dream of becoming a published author come true.

THE GRANDMOTHERS

Mom was strong, and much of that strength, along with many of her best qualities, came from the love poured into her by two remarkable women: her grandmothers.

After my sister and I left for college and moved out, Mom separated from my dad, Jim. With the small sum of money she received in the divorce, she took a bold leap and chased her dream of becoming an author, focusing on capturing family stories. She used every penny to rent a little space in a shop inside the city limits to write her book. She had the book bound and titled it, *Parts of the Tapestry*. She shared it with family and even tried to sell some copies, though that never really came to fruition.

During that time, her focus was on preserving the voices and wisdom of those who came before her. I'm so grateful she did and am thrilled to share some of my favorites here.

She begins the book with these words:

> *I sat beside my grandmothers on many occasions and avidly listened to the stories they'd spin, the advice they dispensed. Their stories need to be saved.*

Parts of the Tapestry

By Darlene Gaynor

One of my favorite passages beautifully captures the essence of her grandparents' lives—the hardships they endured, and the way they chose to love through it all. It reflects not only their resilience but also the quiet, unwavering strength that comes from loving deeply in the face of adversity.

Children don't need to go through things that sad. Life was sad. I knew that from watching my grandma's. It didn't mean the world was going to be perfect just because you got out of bed. You dealt with things. My grandma's taught me a lot. I have to say that my grandpa's taught me a lot too. I was lucky enough to have grandparents

around who didn't strictly raise me, but were here for me
when I needed them. I thank our dear Heavenly Father
for all of my family.

This next poem is a tribute to one of her grandmothers, Rosa. Prayer was important to Mom, and I love that she was reminded of all the ways that she prayed and hoped both for herself and for her friends and family.

Grandmother's Kitchen Prayer

In my grandmother's kitchen,

There was a sweet little prayer.

So, I'd like to take a moment,

And with you these thoughts share.

May the day bring peace, the night time rest,

Ever present health and wealth and happiness.

Friends in abundance, neighbors that care,

May you always have a lovely smile to share.

11/6 detg

The following is a short story about her grandmothers: her mom's mother, Naomi (Grandma Godsey), and her dad's mother, Rosa (Grandma Tuttle). Mom talked about them often; they were more like mothers to her. Both shaped her in meaningful ways. Before she passed, she told me how different they were. Naomi believed in "going to town," while Rosa preferred to stay home, for instance. She learned everything from them.

Grandma Godsey was a lady of today's time, having access to electricity, modern plumbing, a car. She was a little old fashioned, God fearing, and she believed in staying home so she could help her family.

Grandma Tuttle was a lady of yesterday, only getting electricity a few years before I was born. She was born in 1895 in the Cumberland Gap area, and grew up around Bell County, Kentucky. She never wanted a lot of modern conveniences. She felt they were the devil's handiwork. She listened to the radio while she sewed and that was about her only exception to modern conveniences for a very long time. She didn't spout the phrase self-sufficient or minimalism, she just lived it.

She survived the depression and she said having to do without changed your thoughts about living. The family always had huge gardens, a couple of pigs, cows, and beehives. Grandma and Grandpa left their canning jars with friends when they were moving from Kentucky to Tennessee. When he got everyone settled and went back for the rest of their things, they found everything gone. Stolen. They had to go through a winter with their huge family and very little food. She said it made a difference, doing without.

Some of the stories the Grandma's told me are just as fresh today as when they told them. Some are fading just a little. So, in order to do honor to two very important ladies in my life, I will start again on this project of mine. I hope you enjoy our family tapestries.

Mom loved both of her grandmothers deeply, but she always had a closer connection to one, and the same was true for me. We were both especially partial to Rosa.

When Rosa was in her 90s, she was hospitalized. Living in a farmhouse with no indoor plumbing, she needed full-time care. Mom couldn't bear the thought of her returning home alone. So, a few years into her marriage to my dad, she asked to leave our house to care for Rosa. I imagine it broke Dad's heart because he built that house with his own hands, like something out of a fairy tale. He had personally selected the timber from the forest, cut down the trees himself, and milled the wood at a sawmill he restored from an abandoned structure. Mom always told us that he built every inch of our house with love.

We moved in with Rosa, despite the strain I think it put on my parents' marriage. I was three years old, but the memories of that farmhouse are vivid. There was a smokehouse for curing meat, which I found both creepy and completely fascinating. The house was tiny but full of hidden nooks for a curious child to explore. Dad installed indoor plumbing once we moved in and built a big porch where we could play.

I adored Rosa. She ate cornbread soaked in buttermilk, and she smelled faintly of snuff, which dripped from her jaw into hospital-style spit cups she kept close by. As a kid, I thought it was the most amazing thing I'd ever seen. She had a small hymnbook that contained all of my mom's favorite gospel songs. *Wayfaring Stranger, In the Garden, Amazing Grace*—to this day, those songs still remind me of her.

We lived with Rosa for a little over a year. To my understanding, we moved back home because she was becoming less independent and wanted to live with her son. I know my dad was ready to go home, too. After we moved back to Chestnut Hill, I recall visiting Rosa and wanting so badly to ask her all about the world she had lived in a hundred years ago. I didn't yet understand the full weight of all she'd endured, but I knew I was sitting in the presence of a masterpiece.

I never really got the chance to hear Rosa talk about her life story. Thankfully, Mom recorded some incredible tales. I was also lucky to hear a few stories from some cousins who were at Mom's house during her final days. Whether it's the memories themselves, the stories Mom preserved, or the old photos, I feel proud to know what my great-grandmother was capable of. She carried in her mind and body a library of extinct expertise. She knew how to string and dry beans for the winter; how to store turnips, potatoes, and apples in the ground (to make them last longer); how to preserve food in jars; and how to cure meat in the smokehouse. She even dried vegetables on the front porch in the sun. She didn't need a store because she had everything she needed at home on her farm.

And on top of all that, she gave birth to more than ten children, my mom's father being one of them. I can't recall the exact number, but I believe it was twelve.

Here's a story Mom captured about a strange discrepancy in Rosa's recorded age that stuck with her and bothered her for years.

One hundred years ago. 1900. A young wife stands beside her husband, listening to his strong voice. "Rosa will be five this year." she hears him tell the Census Taker.

That's wrong. But she can't correct him in front of another person. She'll correct him later.

1978. Many children and grandchildren later, Rosa Miracle Tuttle is having problems with her Social Security records. They have her one year younger than she is. Still. After all these years. She is not the same age as her brother. Darn. She's one year older.

1995. Deceased. According to Census records, Rosa Miracle Tuttle died just short of her hundredth birthday. According to family records, just short of one hundred and one.

God Bless Rosa Tuttle.

Undated (unusual for mom; she was generally good about dating her stories)

Rosa with my great-grandfather and a few of their many children

Rosa with Mom on her wedding day

Rosa in her nineties, standing in the garden

Me and Rosa, snapping green beans when we lived with her

My sister and I, standing on Rosa's porch. Dried beans,
also known as "leather britches," lined the porch.

Another one of my favorite Rosa stories from *Parts of the Tapestry* talks subtly about some of the pressure and obligation my mom felt from caring for her grandmother. She titled it "Apples."

Apples

DTG August 29, 2000

I've probably mentioned on more than one occasion my Grandma Tuttle was a very frugal woman. She lived through the depression, and as others say that lived through that era, it changes a person. Having to do without will make you very cautious.

Grandma Tuttle went to the garden one morning and didn't come back as quickly as we had expected her to. We went back to the garden and found her on the ground between two watermelons. She had fallen and was in awful pain. Her eyes were closed when we came around the corner, and she was holding the edge of her apron, trying to keep from crying. When she opened her eyes and said she needed to go to the doctor, I knew she was truly hurt. Grandma hated the doctors more than she hated spending money foolishly.

We began to realize how badly she was hurt when we got her to the edge of the porch. She looked up to me and sighed. 'I'd have give a ten dollar bill if I hadn't gone to the garden this morning.'

When we got her to the Emergency Room, they were as gentle as they could be. But Grandma was in her nineties then. And she didn't believe in slacking for any reason. So when the doctor said she'd have to go home without a cast, but keep the weight off her fractured hip bone, we knew it would make for an interesting summer. We had no idea just how interesting though.

Grandma worked almost continuously. She was a firm believer in no idle hands. If you weren't working in the garden, then you were working in the house. There was quilting and canning and freezing to be done, and there was no reason for things not to be completed just because Grandma couldn't move much.

My friend Stella came over one day. We had everything harvestable either frozen, dried, or canned. When the vegetables and fruits were all done, we'd started on the apples in the front yard. Grandma still wasn't happy when those tasks were completed. Her fingers were empty. There wasn't a knife or apples in her hands. She was depressed and upset.

"We could make a few extra dollars selling dried apples this year, if we had a few more apples to put up." She'd look out at the front covered porch, past the screen to the three apple trees we'd already stolen every apple we could. Grandma wanted more apples, and Stella heard the frustration in Grandma's voice when she spoke about apples.

Within a day or so, she'd come back by the house, and mentioned she had a friend who owned a small apple orchard. They weren't going to be able to pick the apples this year and would consider a trade. Apples for Grandma if we picked a few for them too. It sounded like a plan.

My girls were about five and three and thought it was fun to fill up all the baskets and take them back to Grandma's house. The front porch was fair sized but it groaned from the weight of all those apples.

Dried apples, frozen apples, apple jelly, apple butter. Apples here, apples there, apples everywhere. I think we made four, maybe five trips back and forth to the orchard, and Grandma smiled all the while.

Breakfast, getting Grandma and the girls ready for the day. And then peeling apples. Lunch, getting the girls and Grandma ready for the afternoon, and peeling apples. Supper, and getting the girls and Grandma and Jim ready for the evening. And resting for a few minutes. Until Grandma said those apples were not going to wait. We'd better get them ready for drying. Apples.

Some of the cousins came down to visit Grandma during the apple phase. They were appalled. How dare their cousin, the female that was supposed to be taking care of their beloved grandmother, how could she reduce that lovely little woman to work like that? Making her peel all those apples.

All I can say is Grandma was happy. And so were the folks who ended up with apple products of some nature that fall. Any time I run up on a container of dried apples, at the flea markets, or local general stores, I smile. Didn't someone say an apple a day keeps the doctor away? Unless you've tripped on a watermelon in the garden.

My mother's other grandmother, Naomi, faced her own set of struggles. The best way to describe her is as a deeply religious woman—the very image of a sweet, small-town grandmother. Her arms jiggled with the remnants of the church pies she baked and shared. She read the Bible daily and attended church whenever the doors were open. She told us to be kind to our mother and would come to our house to do laundry, often with just enough gas in the tank to get there and back home.

She was, in many ways, the epitome of a righteous woman, but there was one part of her story that didn't quite add up. Her husband, and my grandfather, Monroe, had a mistress. Not only that, but he had two sons with this woman. And Naomi knew. She knew and did nothing.

My grandmother, Helen, was an only child, but I remember one Christmas when Monroe told us that our uncles would be joining us. *Uncles? Plural?* My mom had one younger brother, so I was completely confused. It didn't go well. As a child, I couldn't fully grasp what was happening, but I knew something was wrong. There was tension and strange behavior, and my grandmother wasn't acting like herself. I didn't have the tools to process it at the time, and even as an adult, it has been difficult to untangle those memories.

I'm grateful for Mom's writing, especially that she shared her truth. Her words have helped me sort through the confusion, and more importantly, have given me context about that chapter of our family history. I learned that she, too, was confused and conflicted by the affair. I wasn't alone in feeling like something didn't make sense.

Through her lens, I've come to a more compassionate understanding of Naomi. She was a pious woman. She wore only skirts, studied scripture daily, and lived a life rooted in faith. She also believed that divorcing her husband, even after such a betrayal, would be a sin. That wasn't weakness; it was her version of strength. Her strength was rooted not in confrontation, but in devotion.

Mom (right) and Naomi (center), 1984

Daniel Jr. (Mom's little brother), Naomi, and Mom

Several of the stories about Naomi in *Parts of the Tapestry* highlight the powerful lessons she taught my mom about forgiveness. Even while her husband was building another family, when he brought the children around, she treated them with kindness and respect.

I can't begin to imagine the strength it took to respond that way and the courage it must have required to choose grace over bitterness. Her ability to separate the innocence of the children from the betrayal of the man is something I'm still in awe of.

Here's one of those stories, captured in my mom's own words from *Parts of the Tapestry*.

Grandma Godsey was a tee-totaler. No alcohol allowed. She believed in women wearing dresses. She believed in the power of prayer. And miracles. And the everyday occurrence of family. She loved visiting folks. She always had time to flash her sweet smile or to tilt her head and listen to anybody.

Grandma was a hugger. That might be dangerous by today's standards. Today's society seems to think you live an alternative lifestyle if you hug a female friend or an outrageous flirt if you hug a male friend. She hugged everybody. She saw the good in everyone's soul. It would be nice if that were still possible, but people these days tend to avoid personal contact. No germs. No shared warmth. Avoidance at all costs. Grandma would have not allowed it.

One of the first songs I remember Grandma singing was from the Church of God Song Book. The words were soothing rather than forceful. Melodious rather than entwining.

"I come to the garden alone, while the dew is still on the roses."

That song makes me think of Grandma Godsey. She believed in worshiping privately. Reading your book daily. But she also believed in tongues Talking in tongues is a religious experience not found in all beliefs. Grandma's way of describing it? "It's God talking."

The family attended quite a few churches when I was younger, and I never failed to be amazed at the different practices. One church believed in snake handling. I was never present during one of those meetings.

One believed in getting children truly involved, so their musical content included electrical guitars and drums. With the modernization and popularity of up-beat Christian music, these things have become more common now. They weren't then. There have been churches where the services were almost all sung. I've learned from all of them.

But I probably never enjoyed any experience quite as much as standing beside my Grandma Godsey, smelling the faint smell of honeysuckle perfume on her lacy handkerchief, and listening to the simple words from what I considered her song, "The Garden."

Mom's grandparents carried her through some of the most challenging times in her life. In one of her stories, she refers to Rosa not just as a grandmother but also as a friend and someone who gently taught her how to live and endure. I can only imagine the stark contrast between the chaos of her home life and the calm, steady presence of Rosa's soft hand and quiet wisdom.

Rosa taught her how to plant vegetables, churn butter, and live close to the land. When you've had as many children as she did, I suppose caregiving becomes second nature. But her life wasn't without hardship. Not all of her children survived. One died at birth. Two others were described as "daydreamers"— slow to develop and often lost in their own worlds.

One of them, Doll, suffered a tragic accident. She fell off a porch before the family moved from Kentucky to Tennessee. Doll lived into her forties, but her mind never developed beyond that of a three-year-old. She was tall, strong, and, at times, a physical threat to Rosa, who was small and aging. Eventually, Rosa could no longer care for her. There's a story of the day she had Doll committed to a mental institution. It wasn't a heartless decision; it was an act of heartbreak, a signal of how deeply exhausted she must have been. They came for Doll soon after.

Doll would become a figure etched into both family history and my own name. Mom told me that Burdette was Doll's favorite name to use when she was playing with dolls, and Mom promised to name a child after her. I don't think she could bring herself to name me Doll, so my middle name is Burdette.

In another of Mom's stories, she expresses anger at her mother for not allowing her to attend her grandfather's funeral when he passed away in 1966. This was Rosa's husband. Little was known about Huntington's disease at the time, but I have every reason to believe that it came from his side of the family. I was told he fell often, and it was a fall that ended his life. It sounds hauntingly familiar to the late-stage symptoms of HD.

Still, Mom remembered him fondly. He once bought her a harmonica, though she joked that it may have been to keep her quiet. She told him her dream of performing at the Grand

Ole Opry, and he believed her. I like to picture them walking down a dusty road together, side by side, while she plays the harmonica, her head full of music and dreams.

And that is the story of the grandmothers and the role they played in Mom's life. Those were the early seeds—the small but vital moments—that carried her through. They became the roots of her songs, her stories, her refusal to stop dreaming even when life got hard. I think about Rosa's life sometimes and how remarkable it was to raise 12 children, be married to a man with a rare genetic illness, and still have such a significant impact on my mother.

It's no wonder Mom and I both felt drawn to Rosa. She was a diamond quietly shining, full of wisdom, made strong by pressure. Mom often said that Rosa's faith helped her find joy on the good days and strength on the hard ones. I think of the leather-bound hymnbook my mother wrote about, the one filled with songs Rosa used to sing. *Wayfaring Stranger*, one of her favorites, sings of a person who was just passing through this world. Singing was meditation for Rosa; it was her way of enduring life's challenges and pain. And Mom understood that deep in her bones. She understood the reason Rosa sang.

GROWING UP

Living in an HD family is like being blindfolded while riding a roller coaster. Everything feels upside down and disorienting. You don't know where you're going, and there's no way to get off the ride. Add in denial and memory loss, and you start to lose track of what world you're even living in.

My mom was no exception.

As a child, I had no idea about the abuse she endured growing up. Looking back, there were signs and subtle hints that pointed to a darkness she couldn't speak aloud. Every visit with her family was followed by her anxious questions about our safety, her voice tight with fear and vigilance. Even as an adult, I couldn't comprehend the depth of what she'd been through. Words like "abuse" or even "torture" don't come close.

We were estranged from her parents, Mamaw and Papaw, for most of my life. The times that we were in contact with them were always chaotic. I remember a call to our house when Papaw told Mom they needed to "sell her inheritance," a row of nine rental houses. They claimed they needed the money for medical bills and damages from Papaw's tremors. Papaw hadn't yet been diagnosed with HD, but the symptoms were clearly causing him suffering.

Mom and Dad secured a loan to buy the properties, but they needed her parents to cosign it. When Mom struggled to keep the payments up and the homes occupied, her parents reclaimed the properties. I remember that phone call, too. It happened right when Dad had finalized a plan to sell the topsoil to pay off the loan. I don't know if that was deliberate or just cruel timing. Someone was ready to buy the dirt—kind of like chopping down trees to log them—and that sale would have more than paid for the loan. My dad worked hard to set that up. Not to mention, he had poured sweat and time and care into those homes and felt deeply betrayed. That was the day we were sat down and told, bluntly, by my dad, that we no longer had grandparents.

Dad gave Mom the choice to maintain contact, but he made it clear: His children wouldn't be subjected to that kind of treatment.

Years passed. No cards, no calls. No one came to my basketball games or birthdays. Deep down, I hoped they'd reach out, but they never did.

Eventually, we found out Papaw had been diagnosed with Huntington's disease. This increased my suspicions that his father, Rosa's husband, had HD, even though we'll never know. My dad insisted that Papaw just had a pill addiction, not a real illness. But I've since learned that self-medication is heartbreakingly common for people with HD. Those years must've been hell for everyone, including my uncle, my cousins, and Mamaw. My uncle (my mom's brother) and my aunt were Mamaw and Papaw's next-door neighbors. When Papaw was dying of HD, my uncle was also symptomatic with the disease. They were doing their best to take care of him and themselves. And though I feel for them, I'm also grateful my mother had some distance from the worst of it.

I didn't fully understand how dysfunctional the family truly was until after I graduated from college. By then, Mom's decline was already apparent. She was divorced, homeless, and had just had a terrible altercation with her mother. With nowhere else to go, she came to live with me in Nashville.

It wasn't ideal. I was living with my boyfriend, Matt (who is now my husband), and had to ask him if she could move in with us. It was his first real introduction to our family chaos. I also began using my Employee Assistance Program for therapy—my first taste of counseling. I booked joint sessions for myself and my mom, hoping to understand her better. Mom knew she needed help, so she willingly agreed to go with me. I think this was her first time in therapy, and she opened up immediately.

During these sessions, I learned her father had sexually abused her. I was stunned. Horrified and confused. How could this be true? How could she have allowed us to spend time with them as kids? To stay the night?

I learned in therapy that victims of abuse sometimes displace the trauma or minimize its impact. I wondered if perhaps it was actually someone outside the family who abused her, and she placed the blame on her father instead. But in that moment, sitting beside her, hearing her describe one of the incidents, I believed her. I felt sick.

Still, I needed clarity. I went to see my grandmother, Mamaw. It had been years since I'd last seen her. She didn't seem like a monster. She showed me photo albums and still had pictures of my sister and me on her wall. It was eerie. But I found the courage to ask her, "Did Mom ever tell you she was sexually abused?"

Her answer made me sick to my stomach. She said Mom was lying and had accused some cousins of sexually abusing her when she was little. When I asked about the steps she took to investigate, she became defensive and quickly said, "She was a'lyin."

That was all I needed to hear. I didn't ask another question. I couldn't imagine *not* wanting to understand if someone had hurt my child. I never brought it up again. It was hard for me to stay in contact with her after that. We did end up going to Papaw's funeral, and Mom wanted to reconnect with Mamaw near the end of her life. Still, I was upset that she was so cold and unfeeling when Mom went to her, needing her own mother to be her advocate.

It didn't matter what else my mother told me. I believed her. I loved her. I saw her for who she truly was: a child of trauma, frozen in time, alone in a home without a protector. I respected her more than ever as a survivor.

In the years between learning about the abuse and finally receiving the HD diagnosis, I blamed her struggles entirely on trauma. I didn't realize HD was silently advancing. The changes were gradual, hard to track in real-time. The sad days became more frequent. The forgetfulness crept in. Her joy faded. She struggled with depression, anxiety, and physical health issues. But through it all, she never lost her spirit. She found joy in the little things—in flowers, in sunlight, in music, in the company of those she loved.

Learning her whole story was heartbreaking, but also brought deep understanding. I stopped seeing her as broken. I started seeing her as a woman who fought through more than most ever will. She somehow survived both physical and psychological trauma as a child with no support from her family. On top of that, she spent most of her life battling a disease she didn't know she had. Her diagnosis shifted something in our relationship and how I perceived everything she had been through.

Her response to so much of what she endured was to write. To bring her imagination to life. She was a deeply thoughtful person who struggled so much to understand all the pain and suffering, both emotional and physical, in her life. In writing, she found a tool to not only help center herself but also to escape.

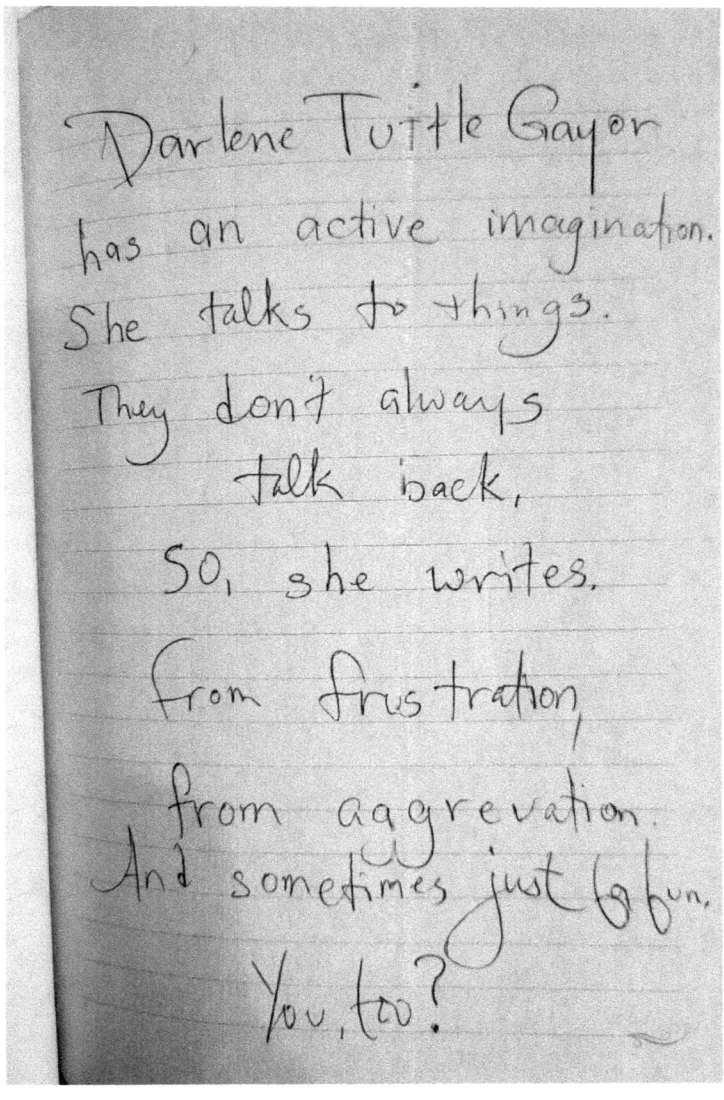

Darlene Tuttle Gayor
has an active imagination.
She talks to things.
They don't always
        talk back,
    So, she writes.
From frustration,
from aggrevation.
And sometimes just for fun.
    You, too?

She was a testament to resilience. She survived what should've broken her. Even in her final years, she kept loving, hoping, and believing in goodness. She saw the best in others, even when she couldn't see it in herself. She didn't focus on the bad. She looked for the good. And I'm so grateful she left that gift with me.

That's her legacy: not just survival, but grace in the face of unbearable hardship. A quiet, powerful reminder that even in the darkest places, beauty and healing are still possible.

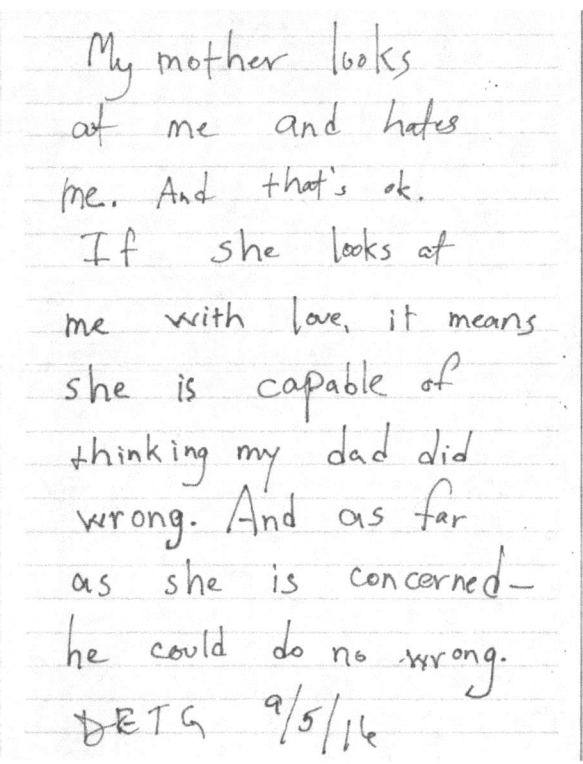

Later in life, she often wrote about her mother and the gratitude she felt that her children and grandchildren never endured abuse as she had.

Family moments before the estrangement. Back row, left to right: Papaw,
Mom (Darlene), Dad (Jim), Aunt Stacy, Uncle Junior.
Front row: Mamaw holding my sister (left),
my cousin Cassandra (middle), and me (right, in blue).

LANEVA

"My characters are real, alive. And I don't think too dry.
Or too sexy. Just right. I hope you'll agree."

— Excerpt from a letter she sent to Avon Books

Mom was always creative and had a deep love for writing. Writing was an escape for her, a refuge. It was a way of expressing the feelings and thoughts she couldn't say out loud. She devoted herself most fully to writing when she set out to become a published romance author. As her daughter, I didn't have the stomach to carry her love stories across the finish line, but I also can't tell her story without including a chapter on the writing she cherished most: *Laneva*.

Laneva now lives in several boxes in my garage—dusty writing tablets, yellowed legal pads stacked high, spiral notebooks filled cover to cover, typewriter pages, and scraps of anything a pen could leave its mark on—all of it telling *Laneva's* love story.

My mother poured her heart into writing and trying to publish *Laneva*. Before Huntington's took hold, she had a vivid imagination, boundless creativity, and big dreams. When I think back on the later stages of her illness, I am comforted by the letters she exchanged with publishers. They remind me that there was a time when her mind was clear, focused, and full of hope. Those letters show a determined, capable writer, one who hadn't yet been taken by the disease.

Here's my favorite letter she wrote to Avon Books, a publisher of romance novels.

Darlene Gaynor
Route 7, Box 230-D
Crossville, TN. 38555

[Name Redacted], Avon Books
1350 Avenue of the Americas
New York, New York 10019

Dear [Name Redacted],

I'd like to join the ranks of Katherine E. Woodiwiss and Johanna Lindsey. I wouldn't mind being compared to Sandra Brown or Beatrice Small. But they're not with Avon Publishing Company.

Several sets of events need to occur before that can happen. With your help, and my persistence, I believe the above can come true.

The first occurrence in this set of events is a forward introduction. To you, by myself, to me. Darlene Gaynor. I hope my work is funny and sexy and serious enough to be considered by your firm.

The second is a guidelines request. This would help me ascertain the rightness of what I have written to what you're requesting. Although, I've read so many Avon books over the years, I feel I have an advantage over writers not as familiar with your books.

It is for this reason I've been forward on a second occasion, and sent three sample chapters of my book, Laneva. I know, she should be called a manuscript, but I'm using visionary techniques and positive enforcement. Think book. Think book. Think book.

I realize, according to Romance Writer's Sourcebook, your company buys mostly agented work. My personal time schedule is running short, though, and I feel it's important for me to bring my work to your attention.

The main reason I've approached Avon Books are your stories throughout the years. Some publishers handle work that's weak and loosely held together with a love scene or two for good measure. Not Avon. I've been involved with many Avon characters over the years. The authors take you with them into the story.

My characters are real, alive. And I don't think too dry. Or too sexy. Just right. I hope you'll agree.

Several objects have been included with this letter to help accomplish the goals set forth. They are as follows:

A self-addressed, stamped envelope for your guidelines. Three chapters from Laneva.

First Chapter – contains prologue and a love scene or two.

Second Chapter – afraid it's one of the weaker chapters, but it's the starting point for the story. It brings together what you've already read with what you're about to read.

Sixth Chapter — just because it's one of my favorites.

I eagerly await your response.

Respectfully,

Darlene Gaynor

I could think of many better things to do than read steamy love scenes that my mother wrote (eww), but I also wanted to include an excerpt from her prized work. It gives a glimpse into the kind of writing style she was evoking in her early thirties: full of heart, hope, and her signature classy style. So, here we go …

> *Eva looked at Cy, admiring the clear eyes that didn't look away from her, and the lips that had told her, in all the ways he could, that he loved her. How could she make this gentle, caring man wait for an answer? But that was what she was going to have to do. She couldn't make a decision concerning her life, her children's life or her husband's life in such a cavalier manner.*
>
> *"Thank you for waiting," whispered Eva gratefully, aware of all she was silently asking of this man.*
>
> *"Thank you for not," came the loving response.*

Okay, enough. You get the idea.

Unfortunately, Avon Books responded with a no. That, however, did not deter my mom. She sent more pitches; I loved seeing her go after the most well-known to me, Harlequin. She also had pages full of other ideas to be developed, constantly thinking of unique romance writing opportunities. There's one in particular that I love; I imagine it came after a visit with me to Nashville:

> *An unusual love - Nashville - Andrew Jackson's love for his wife. Went every morning and spoke with her at her grave site. The couple standing at the pergola were questioning his passion. Would he have been as diligent if she had been alive?*

Writing was truly her passion; it brought her joy and gave her purpose. For me, it's a clear reminder that the journey matters more than the destination. Even though her books never lined the shelves of a local bookstore, she *was* an author. Writing gave her a sense of self and helped her stay grounded through the hardest times.

What excites me most now is writing this book as an opportunity to share her stories with the world, all while raising awareness for Huntington's disease. It feels like the tribute she always deserved.

AVON BOOKS
THE HEARST BOOK GROUP
1350 Avenue of the Americas
New York, N.Y. 10019

3/7/97

Dear Writer,

Thank you for the opportunity to consider your work.

Regretfully, I do not feel that this project is suited to Avon's list. I apologize for the form letter, but with the number of submissions we receive, it is not possible to give a personal response in every case.

Thank you again for your interest in Avon Books; we wish you success in placing your work elsewhere.

Best,

Assistant Editor

March 17, 1997

Ms. Darlene Gaynor
Route 7, Box 230-D
Crossville, TN 38555
U.S.A.

Dear Ms. Gaynor:

Thank you for submitting **LANEVA**, for consideration as a Harlequin Temptation. We have examined it carefully, and while we acknowledge the work you've done, we regret that it does not meet our publishing requirements.

Although we would like to send every author a detailed critique of his or her work, the volume of submissions we receive unfortunately makes this impossible.

We are returning your manuscript to you enclosed, with best wishes for placing it elsewhere. Thanks again for thinking of Harlequin.

Sincerely,

Editorial Assistant
Temptation

AS:mc
TMERG/30/09
Encl.

REMEMBER THE LILIES

Mom adored flowers. When I was a kid, we would zoom around on our Kawasaki four-wheeler, gathering wild bouquets that she'd magically transform into vibrant displays. She always arranged them in mismatched vases, whatever she had on hand, and it somehow worked. As a kid, I never understood the point. I was more interested in the thrill of speed than searching for beauty among bug-filled weeds. What might seem like a detour to others was, to her, the whole adventure.

Looking back now, especially through her stunning photography, I see it differently. Even without modern photography tools, she captured beauty with a sharp eye and deep reverence for nature. Her writing gives me the same gift. Through her words and images, I can piece together what mattered to her. It's like she's still telling me her story one flower, one photo, one page at a time.

After she passed, I started to notice things I'd never truly seen before. I've always loved being outside in nature, and now, it feels more meaningful. The wild bouquets and the spontaneous stops to marvel at a bloom weren't just hobbies for Mom; they were expressions of awe and joy. Now I try to channel that same enthusiasm. I can stare at Queen Anne's lace and lose track of time, fully immersed in the quiet beauty she always saw. It's a strange, wonderful gift, learning to see the world through her eyes.

It's clear to me that admiring the beauty of nature was a way for her to forget the pain. She had an extraordinary talent for finding life in what was often overlooked. I think that's how she felt sometimes, too: overlooked. Writing, photography, vases of flowers—these things gave her something to celebrate. Here's a short poem she wrote and some excerpts from a few others about her love for nature:

I decorate.

We cant escape the fact.

Covering up wounds.

All that crap.

Hiding the holes.

Covering the scars.

where magic

can't be found

in lovely jars.

I decorate.

April 2011

I always think the white ones are the prettiest, until I come down the road and see the lavender ones. And the royal blue ones and the gold and yellow and maroon ones. Iris. Ah.

It goes against my kith. It goes against my kin. Not to collect. To celebrate the beauty God has given to view the flowers together

Queen Anne's lace, sky blue daisies, evergreens. Year after year the beauty never fades, Thank You Lord for beauty unbounding.

While Mom's favorite subject was wildflowers, she also took many pictures of life on our farm. Mom loved living on a farm and being married to a farmer. The photos she took of the landscape evokes the quiet beauty of nature that she so cherished. Here is a sampling of her photography:

Flowers in the fence row on the farm where I grew up

A tree outside the house

Hayfield and pond in front of our barn

Old lumber at Dad's sawmill

Wildflowers—Mother Nature's canvas

The road leading out of our cabin

From the perimeter of the field, looking at the cattle trailer

View of the field from our cabin

Dad taking up hay

This next poem I love because I can see how, even though she was alone, her close friends meant the world to her. She had wonderful friends whom she knew she could count on if she needed them, and they helped her get past all of the lonely times. It reminds me that we are all humans who need connection. I'm grateful to her friends for being there for her.

By Darlene Eva
You got to walk that lonesome valley.
You got to go there by yourself.
There's no one here
Can walk it for you
You've got to walk it by yourself
We find hope in so many places

When we look to the sky.

When we listen to a whip or whill's cry.

When we hear a dear friend say oh my

After you tell them your latest news.

A good friend will tell you the truth.

Not pull any punches when they tell you their views.

A good friend will listen to you all day long.

A good friend will help you sing your sad song.

If that's what you want to do.

A good friend will let you be you.

Mom sitting outside of her public housing, with her flower pots,
about a year before she passed away

LIFE IN SONGS

Most people keep dish towels in their kitchen drawers, but not at our house. Ours were filled with cassette tapes. Mom kept a tape recorder next to the radio, always ready to capture her favorite songs the moment they came on. It was like a sport to her, timing it just right to avoid the DJ's voice at the beginning or end.

Music was one of her greatest loves. She had hundreds of records she'd been collecting since before she was even old enough to pay for them. I'm lucky to still have some of those records in my own collection—a piece of her rhythm, preserved.

This poem hints at her love for music, as well as some of life's other simple pleasures:

I have some problems,

I must admit.

Human to the core.

My favorite song is the one

I'm listening to.

And then the next one's there, and I think,

Ah, that's it.

Couldn't ask for more.

Flowers are the same,

Iris's are my true love.

and yellow roses pretty close behind

And peonies, a girl could lose her mind.

Pinks and whites

and oh my.

And it doesn't stop here.

Cookies, cakes, pies.

Do you see the twinkle in my eye?

So, thank you, Lord, for

everything.

Oh my.

DTG

12/16/12

She never made it to the Opry with her grandfather's harmonica, but she did take a spin at writing songs. It wasn't something she pursued with the same intensity as her other writing. I suppose that maybe because, for her, music was more about listening and escaping than creating. Before I share some song lyrics, here's a poem called *45's Are Still Alive* that represents her love of music.

45's are still alive.

45's are still alive.
33's, 78's, all old records.
Really great.
45's are still alive.

I have a confession to make.
It's not even up for debate.
It's good to let this be known.
My karma, my destiny, my fate.
45's are still alive

There's a collection I've kept all along.
Never let it roam from my home.
They've moved with me through thick and thin.
Lasted longer than friends and kin.
45's are still alive.

Gene Autrey, Dolly Parton and Kansas.
Altos, tenors, sopranos.
All carrying their tunes,
Singing about the moon.
33's, 78's & 45's —
all defiantly alive.

&TG

She moved houses several times later in life, and with each move, pieces of her early writing got lost in the shuffle. I'm sure some of those lost works were songs, and I'm grateful a few samples survived. They're small pieces of her dream that never needed a stage to be real.

I love the following example because it shows her creative process. She worked on this one a lot, refining the verses to get the song just how she wanted it. I don't know if she ever fully finished it. I shortened it to share some of my favorite verses.

We'll go on singing, praising you ever more.
We'll go on singing
Because it's you we adore.
Singing. That's what you'd have us do.
Your love once again, has pulled us through.

I'll go on singing
because you answered my prayers
I'll go on singing cause when I called you were there
Without a doubt, we're only here because of you.
Singing, Singing.

That's what you'd have us do.
I will go on singing
You've brought us through
Singing, singing,
praising you evermore
Singing, singing.
That's what you'd have us do.
Singing, we're only here because of you.

Miracles occur every day. Even when we forget to pray.
Some of us need more healing, more kneeling than others do.

When I have my doubts as to whether everything will be ok, the Lord whispers to   me and says "my child, it will be okay. Let the bad thoughts roll away."

DTG - 11/1/2014

Another piece that really stood out weaved together her faith and love of flowers. It was truly touching and a reflection of how she saw beauty even in the midst of struggle. A gentle reminder that she always believed in something greater, and that we are all part of a bigger, blooming design.

I have been holding on to the past for way too long, I truly have been singing my sad song. It is time to move on. Sad song be gone. I have loved ones to talk to, loved ones to hold, loved ones that can look right into my soul, thank you god.

We are here for a minute and then we fade. As the song says, we'll be blooms far away. Beautiful blooms in the Master's bouquet, so I'm gonna pray. I'm gonna stay to make sure that God has his say.

There's one song that didn't quite hit the mark lyrically but definitely won for funniest title: *"She Killed My Love When She Killed My Truck."* That one was personal. Mom had a bit of a reputation when it came to trucks. Manual transmissions were not her strong suit. She could never quite get the hang of when to shift gears or how to tell if the ground was too soft to drive on. I have vivid memories of sitting in fields with a stalled truck, long before cell phones existed. Mom would always stay with the vehicle, and one of us kids would be sent off running to find Dad and the tractor.

Honestly, it still feels like a great country song in the making.

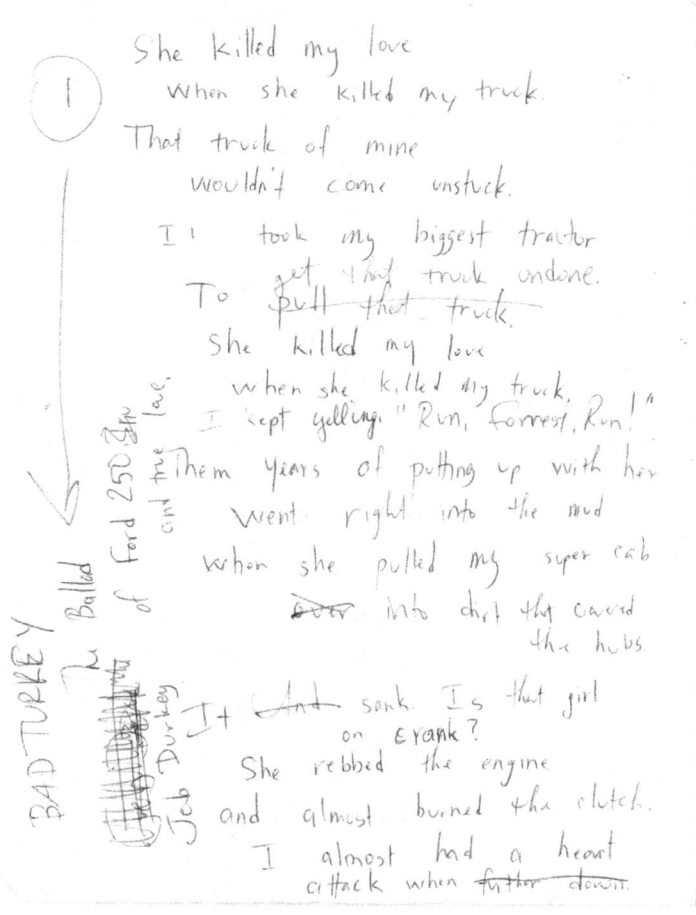

This last piece speaks to her unshakable spirit.

I was a little bit short of money
I was a little bit short of time
I was just thinking if I had both

would it not be sublime
Damn, if I had both that would be just fine
But I don't
I did the best I could
from where I stand
I stood where I was supposed to be

Somehow, despite everything, she knew she was doing the best that she could. I think that's what kept her going. It's not that hard, really, to just give up when things get tough. My mom is a testament to what it means to endure life's most difficult moments with grace, and I'm grateful to have these song lyrics to remember her by.

COPING STRATEGIES

Life, for my mom, was often a sharp contrast between the beauty she saw everywhere and the sadness she quietly carried. She could find wonder in the simplest moments. Yet underneath it all was someone constantly working to survive her own pain.

Her marriage meant so much to her. When she and my dad divorced, something in her shifted. The writing from that period is too much for me to read. The depth of heartbreak on the page is overwhelming. I can feel her isolation, her grief, her sense of being irrelevant. The memories tied to that time are intense.

She was alone and broken, yet still she wrote. Writing was her saving grace. She tried to process the pain the only way she knew how: by putting it into words.

Here's some of her work from that chapter in her life.

I thought you were the perfect one for me
Strong and true
and brave.
I thought I'd love you til the grave.
I thought we'd hold hands,
grow old together

on the front porch
in our rocking chairs.
Guess I was wrong.
So wrong.

The next one, Will-o-Wisp—I love that it's this mysterious, mythical creature. It feels meditative to me, like she's calling on the energy of the universe. This was something she was deeply connected with, which I think helped her feel a sense of security when dealing with all the pain.

Will-o-Wisp
What have I become?
No one wants to say my name.
What have I done?
To be so ready to take the blame?

All those things I didn't do,
Cause I was so true to you.
My heart has turned to blue.
At least for the time being.
And no immediate changes am I seeing.

Desolate and all alone.
No one's waiting for me at home
You've not been there in such a long time.
Why should that thought make me cry?
Whipper wheel just said goodbye.
Will-o-wisp you still make me cry.

During this time, her writing progressed from questioning to anger to a resolve to not let this situation define her. She still existed as a writer, a mother, and a woman, despite the immense pain she held inside.

My purpose is … to remember what my smile looks like

Like a gentle evening rain bringing strength
again and again
Let it go.
Let it melt quickly like late March snow.
Let the smile send the ache away.
Smile

She would often write these little messages and thumb tack them next to some gorgeous landscape picture or wildflower scene she had photographed. A reminder that there is still beauty in suffering.

when you're in that frozen mode - try and think
you've asked God to move your footsteps
so that means you probably need to move your feet.

God's imperfect people are walking all around.
God's imperfect people.
I am surprised.
Their numbers do abound.
But with this love and grace,
we are not just living,
We have begun to thrive

Some of the most painful pages to read are the ones where she's processing my father's infidelity. Her words hit me hard:

Of all the things I thought you might do, I never thought that of you.

Followed by:

Others told me, right from the start, don't fool with him—he'll break your heart.

It's incredibly difficult to relive the pain she felt through her words. I can feel the heartbreak in her phrasing. Even the handwriting itself shifts; it's more frantic, rushed. The emotional weight is evident not just in what she said, but also in *how* she said it. You can see where it hurt the most.

How do I begin to heal? The devastation was quite real.

That line in particular stuck with me. While reading, my emotions began to mirror her penmanship—unsteady, heavy, raw.

But then her writing shifts.

She starts writing about my nieces and how their presence pulled her through. How their laughter, their little hands, their light brought her back from the edge. I felt the change as I read. The tone lifted. Her focus shifted. I had traveled the entire arc of emotion with her, from devastation to renewal.

This was how she coped. This was her way of surviving.

Yes, life is painful. My mother taught me that there are things we can pour our energy into that help us heal. Flowers.

Music. People we love. Even in her darkest moments, she found beauty. And when she couldn't find it, she created it. That's a lesson we could all learn.

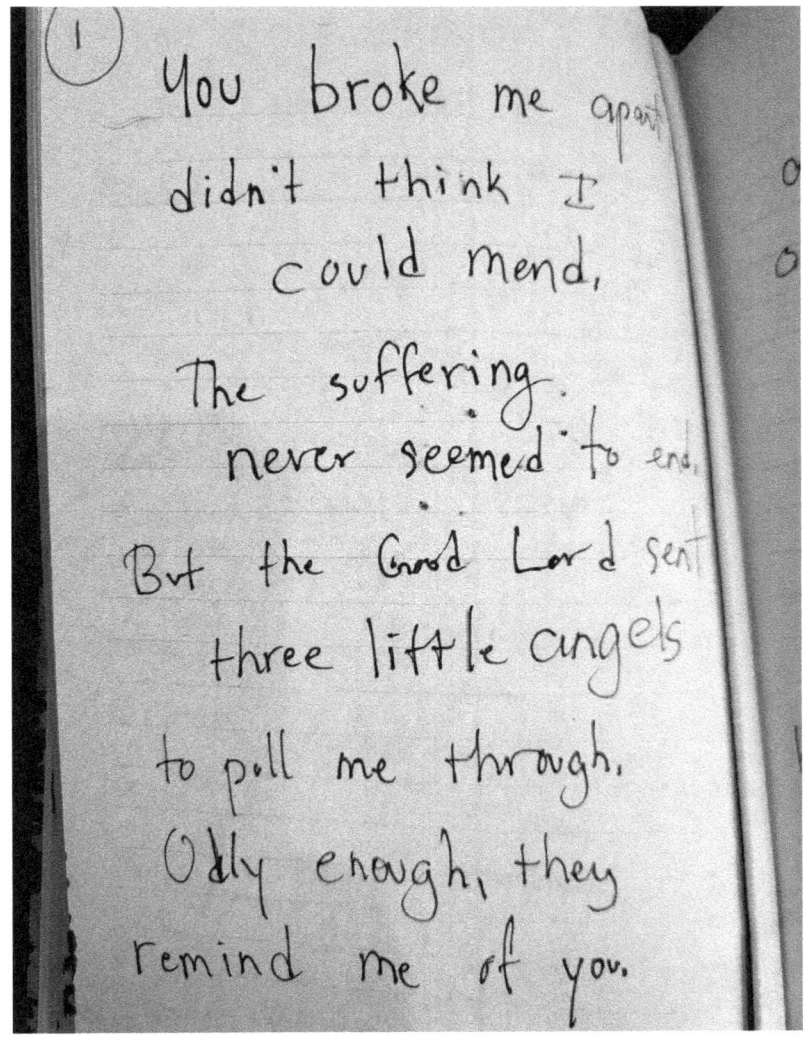

ADVENTURES WITH MOM

At times, living with her felt like stepping into a child's dream. She created something that could only be described as a kind of wonderland—Darlene's Adventures instead of Alice's. We called it *the material room.*

That's where she earned the nickname Granny Buttons.

The walls were lined with shelves so sturdy that not even a Category 5 hurricane could have knocked them over. The shelves housed heaps of fabric, lovingly gathered from the sale racks of Walmart's fabric department, each piece full of possibility.

Beside the shelves stood filing cabinets, overflowing with sewing patterns for clothes she dreamed up more often than she sewed. That room was more than just a collection of fabric and thread, it was her creative sanctuary. In this space, imagination and material came together, and she quietly stitched her dreams into being.

In front of the window sat her record player, surrounded by crates stacked on crates, overflowing with vinyl she'd collected over the years. And then, the crown jewel of the room: a Macintosh computer from nineteen eighty-something. I'm not sure if a friend gifted it to her or if she stumbled on it at a yard sale, but somehow, we had one.

We were obsessed with the green-screen version of *Jeopardy.* If you had (or can imagine) a video game made in the 1980s, that's what this was. The questions would display on the screen with text answers and a "ding ding!" if you got the answer right or a "wah wah!" if you got it wrong. It was the only part of the computer we were allowed to touch. She made it very clear: hands off everything else. That old Mac wasn't just for games; it was where she wrote *Laneva*. And to her, that story was sacred.

Our cousins and a select few friends knew all about the magic hidden in the material room. We'd spend hours designing outfits, embellishing them with buttons and brooches Mom had no doubt gathered from local yard sales. Glamour shots didn't require a real camera, just our imaginations. She would drape fabric around us with effortless grace, turning scraps into gowns. In those moments, we felt like royalty.

That room was her escape—a space to create, to dream, to breathe. It was her peace corner before peace corners were a thing, and, often, it became ours too.

But as I got older, the magic slowly gave way to melancholy. I didn't realize it then, but my view of my mother was shifting. The woman I'd seen as brilliantly creative and wicked smart now looked more like a hoarder who rarely dusted. The aspiring writer I admired began to appear lost, detached from reality.

I knew she was still the same woman beneath it all—intelligent, imaginative, one-of-a-kind—but something was changing. Was it me? I began to wonder if the version of her I'd always loved was just a product of my childhood wonder. Or if, perhaps, both could be true.

I remember studying abroad in college, wandering through the most incredible museums across Europe, and wishing she were there with me. I brought home a few posters from my travels, imagining how thrilled she'd be to see them. One was a Gustav Klimt print I bought at a museum in Germany. I thought she would enjoy how he used symbolic imagery to depict emotions. When I gave them to her, she said all the right words, yet I didn't *feel* anything behind them. She seemed sad and distant.

Later, one of her closest friends told me she once offered to pay for a trip for Mom to go to Europe, and Mom turned it down. That wasn't like her. As I mulled this over, it went from seeming odd to making me question everything. Maybe I'd imagined the woman I thought she was. Maybe the version of her I carried with me wasn't real.

But now, when I look at the stacks of records she loved, the photos she took with such care, and the brilliant words she left behind, I know I didn't imagine her. That *was* my mother. The posters still hung on the wall, even if she could no longer summon the excitement for them, and that meant something.

She may not have been able to show it later in her life, but her spirit remained, tucked away deep inside, and evident in all the creativity she left behind. And I've come to believe that everyone deserves a space like the material room—a place to dream, to create, to hold onto who they are, even when life tries to take everything away.

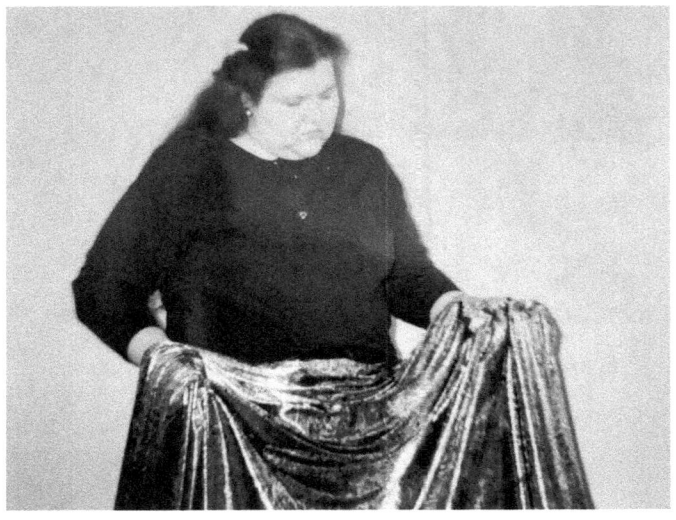

Mom with one of the many pieces of fabric from the material room

*Four-wheeler, stuck in the mud. She always had a way
of finding the soft spots in the field.*

FACING LIFE'S CHALLENGES

When Mom was young, she was a great student, but her parents didn't have the means to send her to college, so she went straight into the workforce. Although Mom loved working, staying employed was often a struggle. Still, the rewards of her efforts—both emotional and tangible—kept her motivated.

Her first major purchase was also her most prized possession: a 1987 Jeep CJ-5. She was so proud of it. My sister and I still have it, though it's seen better days. Dad lovingly added a wooden box in the back where the dogs could ride, eventually turning it into a hunting Jeep. But in the beginning, it was hers. She earned it, she owned it outright, and she cherished it deeply.

Most of the work she did was administrative, though she also picked up shifts at the most charming little Southern restaurant in our town, the Bean Pot. It was decorated in full Gatlinburg flair with a Dolly Parton-meets-country-roadhouse vibe. Autographed photos of country music stars lined the walls, stained by years of smoke and storytelling. It was there, driving that CJ to work and flashing her signature charm, that she met her future husband, my dad.

Life began to pull her in a different direction. Pregnancy, raising children, and eventually moving to care for her grandmother meant she had to put her career on hold. That resulted in a long gap in employment, though never a gap in purpose or love.

Mom doing administrative and sales work (1980s)

She always wanted to do her best, but working was a challenge for her. Over the years, she held jobs as a waitress, flower delivery driver, gas station attendant, census clerk, teacher's assistant, secretary, guest sales associate, and the list goes on. I think she was fired from almost every job imaginable. And when she wasn't fired, she quietly allowed herself to "retire early" once the reality of her difficulties became too clear to ignore.

The hardest one for me was Meals on Wheels. It was basically a step above a volunteer position. I knew that she couldn't take on work that was physically or mentally difficult. But I was frustrated that she couldn't even do something as simple as walking an already prepared meal into a home. Knowing what I know now, it pains me that I felt this way. Her career path, in many ways, mirrored the progression of her disease. In the early years when she worked, the mistakes were small. But it was never easy, and over time, it became increasingly difficult for her to focus, and her fatigue kept her from completing even simple work tasks.

I remember feeling deeply embarrassed in third grade when she helped my teacher grade papers; she couldn't follow the answer key and marked a bunch of tests wrong. She was starting to lose focus and was getting confused more easily. She also gained a significant amount of weight, which brought its own challenges. My classmates were already making fun of her appearance, and now I had to worry about whether she was capable of functioning. It was a lot to carry for a kid.

By then, I had already figured out that homework help was out of the question. Whenever she tried to assist, it often ended in her yelling at me when I told her I didn't think she was right, or else worse grades when I actually followed her advice. She was struggling to communicate, and I think she felt overwhelmed when she couldn't understand something. I began to feel very alone, realizing that if I wanted something done right, I had to do it myself.

That pattern stayed with me for a long time. I've spent years trying to retrain my mind through leadership development, meditation, and inner work, all in an effort to overcome those early, deeply ingrained beliefs about trust, control, and support.

As time passed and her abilities declined, her jobs changed, too. She transitioned from creative and administrative roles into labor-based work, although the physical demands became increasingly difficult due to her health and the weight she carried. Still, she kept trying. And in the midst of it all, there was a kind of resilience in her—a quiet, aching determination to keep showing up, even as the pieces of her life that held her together were starting to slowly slip away.

Before we knew Huntington's disease was part of our story, I created my own version of reality. It was one shaped by frustration, confusion, and growing resentment toward my mother. Learning that HD ran in our family wasn't exactly a relief, but understanding the *why* behind her decline was. It gave meaning to her actions that, to me, had felt like failures.

As hard as it was to watch her struggle to hold down a job, I've come to find comfort in the fact that she never stopped trying. She showed up, over and over again, despite the odds.

I did everything I could to help her find work that she could manage, long before we knew about Huntington's. When she came to live with Matt and me in Nashville, we poured our energy into helping her build a new life. We spent hours working on her résumé, reaching out to companies to see if they were hiring, and giving her tips for interviews. I even conducted some mock interviews with her so that she could practice and feel more comfortable with the process. But after being late to several interviews or getting lost trying to find the locations, we finally gave up on that route.

Eventually, we found a job for her at the Goodwill down the street. I knew they hired people with disabilities, and at that point, I had started to accept that something deeper was going on. She was happy—so genuinely happy—to have work. But it was physically demanding, and she began telling me she was tired and sweating a lot. In my usual "power through" mindset, I gave her Tylenol and encouraged her to keep going.

After a few months, she told me she wanted to move back in with my sister. She said she missed her grandkids, and I knew she did. The reality was that she also needed a break from *me*. I was tough on her.

Just a few short weeks after moving, she walked into my sister's house pale and crying. My sister was terrified and rushed her to the hospital. The doctors immediately ordered an ambulance transfer to the nearest trauma center. That's when we learned she had a tumor on her kidney that had ruptured. She was diagnosed with kidney cancer. This was about seven years before her HD diagnosis.

The medical team told us she must have been in serious, debilitating pain for months. I was gutted. The woman I'd been pushing to power through had been quietly suffering. And yet, she never yelled at me. She never blamed me or told me how wrong I was. Instead, she stayed grateful for the home and the job, despite her suffering. That's the kind of person she was: selfless, gracious, and full of quiet strength.

Looking back, I'm honored to have had a mother who could put others before herself, even when it cost her so much. Her spirit continues to teach me about kindness, patience, and what it really means to love. Of course, there's a part of me that wishes she had put herself first sometimes, and I know that she tried, but I don't think she was fully capable.

The cancer diagnosis added a new layer to everything. I began to wonder: Had she been changing all along because her body was quietly battling this disease? Was cancer the reason she had struggled so much with work?

After the tumor was removed, she was able to participate in a clinical trial to monitor for recurrence. It was a huge relief, especially since she didn't have health insurance. The trial not only offered medical oversight but also gave her access to consistent care.

During one visit with her oncologist, I asked whether she could return to work after having a kidney removed. His answer wasn't what I'd hoped for. He said she could work, leaving me wondering what was wrong with her. Officially, on paper, she could work, but I knew that she couldn't. I had pushed her to keep working, trying to believe she could, when in reality, it was breaking her down. I felt a fresh wave of guilt. Years earlier, she'd asked for help applying for disability, but I couldn't stomach it. I didn't want to see her as someone who couldn't work. I wanted her to be "normal," and I convinced myself she just wasn't trying hard enough.

I believed trauma had worn her down, and that being around people might bring her back to life. But that wasn't the full story. Deep down, I was also tired—tired of being the one who shared money, managed logistics, and made sure she was okay. At the time, I didn't fully grasp that even a few hundred dollars a month from disability would have changed her life. She knew it. She understood her limits. But I wasn't ready to.

Even during her cancer treatment, there was still no mention of Huntington's. The clinical trial focused on monitoring the cancer through scans and follow-ups, but it also provided her access to Vanderbilt and a broader care team. That extra attention was a gift; logistically, it was a challenge. Each appointment meant a full day off work for me: two hours of driving, several hours more spent sitting in waiting rooms, and walking to and from scans and doctor visits. The cost added up, not just in money, but also in time, gas, and energy. It wasn't easy, but we managed it.

Eventually, we found a transportation service that could drive her to Vanderbilt, and I'd meet her there for some of her appointments. Over time, that turned into just meeting her for lunch. Then there were times I couldn't make it at all. The days she had to take the van were long and exhausting for her, made worse by her growing struggle with personal hygiene. She didn't have the energy or will to shower, brush her teeth, or care for herself in basic ways. I think sitting shoulder to shoulder with strangers in tight spaces made it even harder emotionally. She missed many appointments, but she always tried her best, mostly because she hoped she'd get to see me.

If I could wave a magic wand and do it all over again, I would have pushed for testing for Huntington's much earlier. I would have asked for help. I would have tried harder to understand instead of retreating in frustration. Without a diagnosis, it just looked like she had given up on herself. Hindsight is 20/20, I know, but at the time, I didn't know she was sick. I thought she was choosing not to try. And that lack of understanding shaped so much of my reaction, which was to push. Push her to work, push her to doctor's appointments, push her to take care of herself.

For most of my life, I believed I had to work harder because my mom couldn't. Someone had to provide. At times, I felt angry. Ashamed. Burdened. The pain of each job loss, each disappointment, cut deep enough that I sometimes had to detach just to cope. I know she felt that pain, too. But she kept going.

Through everything, she still managed to find joy, friendship, and love. She volunteered with local organizations and cared deeply for the children at Crab Orchard Elementary. Long after my sister and I were kids, she ran a store at the school where the students could earn points in class to buy little toys and trinkets. She was always at the thrift store, searching for items for her store. Crab Orchard is a rural school where most of the population lives below the poverty line. She loved being able to bring some joy to the kids. She always found a way to help, even when she had nothing. With no money to work with, she still managed to organize senior citizen coffees on a shoestring budget. No matter how bad things were, there was always someone she could show up for. That became her job, in the absence of an official title.

Life for families affected by Huntington's is uniquely difficult. Because of the genetic nature of the disease, care often falls to those who are also at risk or already impacted. In our case, we were lucky not to inherit HD, but that didn't make caregiving any easier. Raising our own families while caring for Mom was overwhelming. I constantly struggled with wanting to be there for her and needing to be there for my children. Working full-time, parenting, and caregiving was a herculean effort.

Thankfully, my sister and I were able to tag-team the support. I helped financially as best I could; she gave more of her time. We made it work, imperfectly but with love. A lot of what I've had to process over the years is simply accepting that we did the best we could with the information available to us at the time. If I could offer advice to other families, it would be this: Trust your gut. Advocate for your loved ones. There *are* people and programs that can help, but you have to fight to find them.

Certificate of Appreciation from the school where she volunteered

Crab Orchard Seniors Club will be meeting Tuesdays at 10am in the Old Head Start Building. We will be in the building next to the Mayor's office. We will be planning future activities and games.

Refreshments will get us started, and we plan on finishing by 2pm. Come be a part of the community, voice your opinions, and gently pick on your neighbor. AARP states 55 and above is considered a senior, so we are going with those numbers. Darlean and Darlene plan on being there. We think Norma and her fella might perform on the karaoke machine. Come on and join us for singing and companionship. If you need further information, call Darlene at

The Seniors Club flyer she created

THE DARK SIDE OF HD

M om didn't have much support growing up. The coping mechanisms she developed were formed in survival mode, not in the context of a nurturing environment. She lived her life not to thrive, but simply to survive. Although she often shared stories of her mother's abuse, she still ended up repeating some of those patterns with us. Her anger was mostly reserved for her family. When we didn't listen, she might raise her voice like any parent, but when pushed too far, she struggled to regulate her emotions. Brooms were broken across the kitchen floor. She yelled, threw things, and once the storm passed, she often gave us a heartfelt apology.

By the time I was 14 or 15, I'd had enough of being pushed around. One day, I shoved her back. My sister was horrified, but I didn't feel any remorse. I was tired of being hit. Tired of feeling helpless. And, in that moment, I realized I was stronger than her. I wasn't going to be hurt anymore.

We learned to anticipate the cycle. Some triggering event, like an argument or a bad memory, would lead her to binge eat, pass out for hours, and then wake up angrier than before. A phone call from her father or a comment from my dad could send her spiraling, and my sister and I were left caught in the fallout. We adjusted our behavior to avoid it. We could read her moods like a weather forecast. Some days were good, and some were stormy. We learned how to calm her with a hug or a kiss, or how to quietly retreat without her noticing. She could shift from joy to fury in seconds. It often felt like living with someone who had bipolar disorder.

She often felt remorseful about how she treated us and would profusely apologize. But words are nothing without actions. Her apologies didn't stop the outbursts.

As she aged, the mood swings and contentious behavior became more intense. In college, I began receiving calls from others about erratic behavior. There were outbursts at the farmers market, arguments with friends, and even altercations with others. We always braced ourselves for the inevitable friendship breakups. The people who stuck around long enough began to see the pattern. Her closest friends learned to navigate the storm: the sudden anger, the confusion, the emotional whiplash. There was a Dr. Jekyll and Mr. Hyde dynamic that, at the time, we couldn't explain—but it was there, and everyone could see it. More than once, she was admitted to inpatient care. It became clear her ability to self-regulate was deteriorating. The combination of Huntington's disease and unprocessed trauma had created a brutal internal storm.

After college, the crises became more frequent. She confided in me more than once that she didn't want to live. She was admitted to mental health facilities for suicidal thoughts. I always hoped she'd receive the support she needed in these facilities because I didn't have the capacity. Taking care of her in that way was more than I could give. I was barely an adult, studying at university on an academic scholarship and building a life and future career for myself. I often struggled with friendships in college because I was secretly dealing with the burden of knowing that my mother was lonely, depressed, and falling apart. I didn't know how to help her. I tried, from afar, to nudge her toward medical care. But without insurance, the system was brutal and a punishment we didn't ask for. When you need help and can't pay, there are layers of shame that come up, making it difficult to ask for and receive the care you need. Charity is a hard word to swallow.

She did eventually find help through unconventional treatment options. One of these was a facility called the Sunshine Center, which was grounded in a twelve-step program. I never joined her, but I saw how much it helped. That community gave her some light. Looking back, knowing what I now know about Huntington's, I'm amazed she managed to keep going. Even more remarkable was the way she documented her pain. Her words on paper allow me to remember her beyond the illness, to honor the woman beneath all the suffering.

As I came to terms with my trauma, I began my own recovery. My life challenges left me at a crossroads, and I knew I needed help. Like Mom, my path led me to a twelve-step program. I sought therapy and was told that I could benefit from a program called Al-Anon. My dad was an alcoholic, and Al-Anon is a group therapy program for family and friends of alcoholics. My deeper wounds came from my relationship with my mother, but confronting the trauma from my dad's alcoholism allowed me to start healing myself, one step at a time. I attended my first meeting and immediately felt at home.

The irony of generational trauma is that it often lands you right back where you started, repeating the negative cycles you're trying to break free from. The only difference is whether someone points you toward healing. I stayed involved with Al-Anon on and off for years and gained so much beneficial advice. I felt less alone in that community.

Once I had children, new issues surfaced. However, these issues were physically present when they manifested in my children's behavior. My oldest child was experiencing some issues at preschool, which prompted me to seek help in understanding how to support her. The joke was on me. It wasn't my daughter who needed help. I learned that her very early anxiety was likely due to my own anxiety showing up. The therapist gently explained to me that anxiety in a child that young is typically learned from a parent. She was right.

In my effort to escape the dysfunction of my past and build a better life, I had developed survival mechanisms that wired my brain to "always on" mode. I could plan ahead, anticipate others' needs, and see the big picture, something great for corporate strategy but terrible for emotional presence. I couldn't even name my feelings. These behaviors helped me survive, but did not serve me as a mother.

I left that therapy session with a feelings chart, some reading recommendations, and a fierce determination to understand myself. Like my mother, I had turned to yelling, self-criticism, people-pleasing, and throwing things when I was overwhelmed. It has been nearly a decade since that session. Today, I'm proud of the progress I've made. I journal, express gratitude, breathe deeply, and practice positive affirmations. The first real step toward healing was seeing the disconnect between how I viewed myself and how others experienced me. That mirror changed everything.

I'm grateful that I was able to find help and that I committed to doing the work to heal my trauma, not only for myself but for my kids as well. I'm grateful that Mom was open to receiving support from inpatient facilities and leaning on her friends and family for support. She managed to keep the suicidal thoughts at bay. Others in her family were not so lucky.

Her brother, who also had HD, committed a murder-suicide, taking both his own life and my aunt's life.

I genuinely believe that my mom's writings are what saved her, what kept her relatively sane. Though the disease still took her life in the end, the words that she put to paper were a healing balm in her darkest moments.

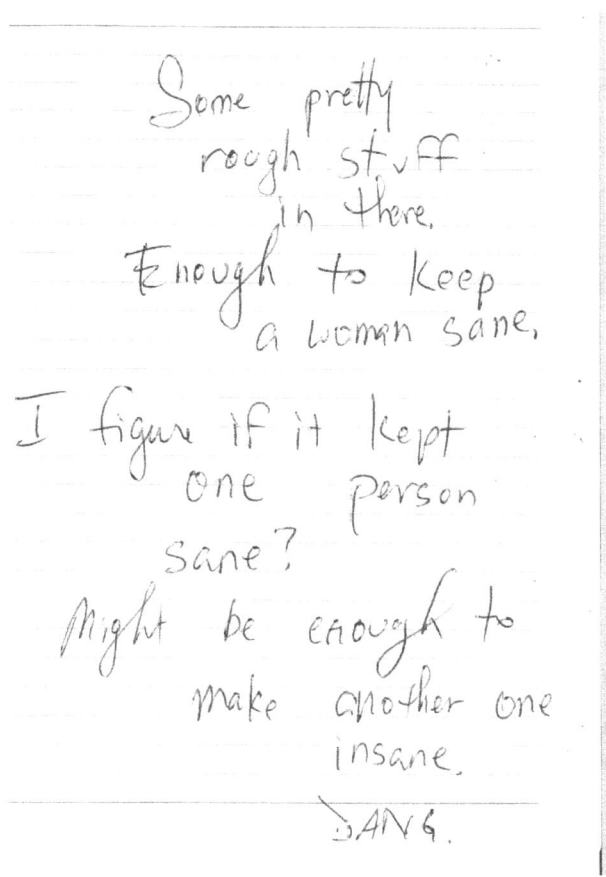

One of Mom's writings around the time
she visited the Sunshine Center

Suicide Prevention

Everyone is invited to attend an informational session provided by the Tennessee Suicide Prevention Network on Monday, August 13th from 6:00-8:00 pm at the Crossville Church of Christ, 423 North Main Street. This will not only provide statistics, warning signs, etc. but will also provide every person with some training on how to respond to a person who may be struggling with these feelings.

A pamphlet I found in her belongings

Resolved   5/20/2013

Let it go.
Let it go
just like
white ice and snow.

Let it rain.
Let God's tear drops
disolve all the pain.
Let it rain.

Smile!
That's a treasure
we haven't felt
for a while.

If the joy
is the same?
Let's not refrain.
Smile.
Nashville. TN.

*A poem from when she lived in Nashville. Here she is working
to find the joy that helped bring her out of the darkness.*

GRANNY BUTTONS

There was only one thing Mom loved more than being a mother, and that was being a grandmother. In the later years of her battle with Huntington's, it became harder for her to express that love in words, but she didn't need to. We all knew. Her love for my nieces pulled her through the darkest moments. I have no doubt about that. Children know when they're loved. They felt it from her deeply and loved her right back.

She loved my children just as much, but sadly, she didn't have the same time with them. By the time they were born and growing, the disease had progressed, and I was more cautious. I couldn't leave her alone with them because it wasn't safe. She couldn't care for herself, let alone little ones. But for my sister, Mom was still an option, and she was so grateful for that time. They were good for each other. It was healing, even when it was hard.

My sister and I grew up helping care for a grandmother, our dad's mom. She suffered a stroke more than a decade before we ever met her. She was paralyzed on one side and needed constant support. We were given a big responsibility at a young age, regularly checking in to make sure she was okay. Looking back, I'm grateful for that experience. I think it helped shape our compassion.

For my nieces, it helped them to show up for their grandmother in their own way, too. They were lucky enough to have her live with them on and off throughout their lives. It was a blessing, though not always easy. Still, they had time with her, and that time mattered.

When my oldest daughter was born, Mom gathered her cousins (my nieces) and helped them create a beautiful handmade book just for her. The first page states that it is a "heart made production" and explains that the book is a collection of art to welcome Ellie (a name we initially considered; ultimately, we decided to go with Eleanor) to the world. There is a picture of a family tree decorated by her toddler cousins, and underneath, it says, "We love you unreservedly." There are also poems written by Mom telling her how loved, blessed, and cared for she is. It's a bit cheesy and very sweet, and Eleanor treasures it. She knows it came from her grandmother and that it's full of love.

I like to think that Mom channeled all her lonely feelings from childhood and the abuse she endured and the support she lacked into creating something beautiful. She knew, deep down, that children need to be loved, cared for, and wanted. Unfortunately, Mom didn't have the ability to make a book like this for my other two kids. But in true Mom fashion, she did leave behind many writings, and now I'm combining them to continue documenting the tree. So they, too, will know just how deeply they were loved.

Cousin art in the book given to Eleanor from Granny Buttons

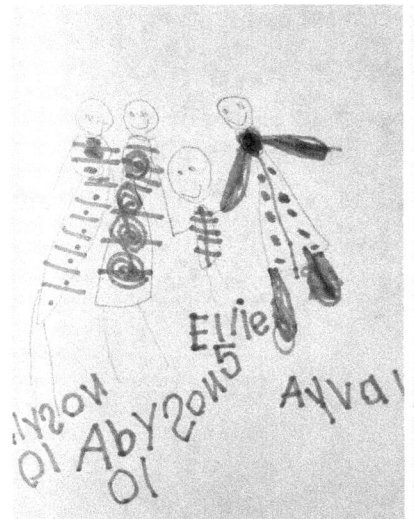
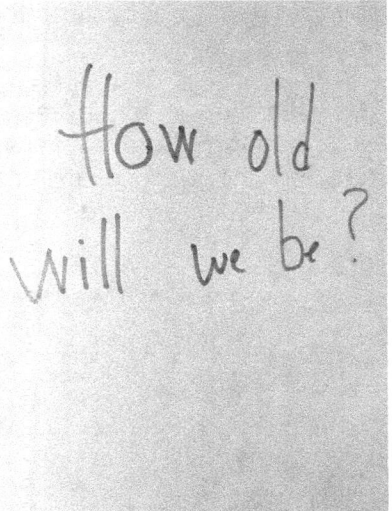

More art calling out how many years apart they were and
what to expect in the future

Grandma's Pardon

Alyson is running at me,
jumping right into my lap.
Annie's right behind her
and I can tell there's about to be a scrap.
Alyson, did you do that?"

She looks up at me and smiles
that beautiful grandchild smile.
Her mom is looming in the back.
"You know you have to be good
and do like your mother says."

She leans over and rests her head against my chest.
I think that means, in almost two time,
"Grandma, I tried to do my best."
Mom doesn't understand the almost two time right
now.

She used to, when she and her sister spoke it.
She has forgotten that time, trying to be the make my
children be good children mom in make my children
be good children time.

A poem Mom wrote for my nieces (page one)

Grandma's Pardon - page two

Ayva has discovered pens and refrigerator doors.
Adyson has discovered she like standing at the
screen door and watching all that's going on.
Annie looks around to make sure all three can still be
found. They can. She's doing a good job.
Can't tell her that though, it would go to her over
twentyone head.

Alyson, Addie and Ayva know that if they really get in
a fix, Grandma's lap can save ya.
Yep. That simple.

A poem Mom wrote for my nieces (page two)

Mom with my nieces on her 50th birthday

Granny Buttons wanted everyone to have a little silliness and happiness in their lives, especially her grandkids. I know she wishes she could've stuck around a lot longer. This next piece, titled "A Mother's Worries," is a reminder of how much she cared about us and worried if she had raised us right. A parent may never know the full extent of the wisdom they pass on to their children. Sometimes, by the time we realize all that we learned, they are gone. So I hope my mom knows that she taught me so much about being a loving and compassionate person. Life growing up with her was far from perfect, but I know she cared. And now I'm trying my best to remind my kids of the lessons my mom taught me about happiness and caring for others.

Jessica Marie

What did I teach you?
Did I at all succeed?
Did I teach you to ask the
    for guidance when you truly
        have needs?
    Did I make you aware of Compassion?
Did I teach you grace of deed?
    Did I forget to mention
    I keep you _____ need?

Laughter, living, caring, compassion. Patience, Regard,
Hope, and Health and happiness. And an occasional ___ day.
    Good Lord and Heavenly father, as I ask for your
    _____ all the time could you look out for
    _____ daughters and I know
    you know are a gift of mine? And their dads.
Laughter, loving, caring, compassion.
    _____
        keep them _____
        ___ as pie. Who ___ that
            Never ___ said it'd be hard?
                ___ who ever said it'd be hard?

Where are the peremiters?
Exactly how far can you go?
Writing and travelling and searching.
Is there anyone out there who knows?

Heartfelt sigh.

What exactly did I teach you?
Did I at all succeed?
All of these questions. Lord,
can cause a
mothers scared heart to bleed.
Laughter, loving, caring, Compassion, Regard.
Hope aND health and happiness.
And an occasional ta dah!

Darlene Gaynor
3/27/08

HER PAIN AND SUFFERING

After our first child was born, my husband and I decided to purchase larger life insurance policies. As part of the application, we were asked whether we had any known genetic conditions in our families. This was four years before my mother received her HD diagnosis in 2019. I felt incredibly confident that I did not have Huntington's disease at the time. Since a neurologist once told my mother it was unlikely she had HD, I took it at face value.

So, when filling out the paperwork, I marked "yes" to a family history of HD but reassured them that a neurologist had "ruled it out." Looking back now, I realize how naïve that was. The only way to definitively rule out Huntington's is through a genetic test.

I'm embarrassed now that I didn't dig deeper. That misplaced trust delayed our understanding of what was really happening. After Mom received the official diagnosis, I requested her previous medical records from the local neurologist she had seen a few years prior. In a 2017 visit, the doctor noted she reported a "new complaint"—numbness and tingling in her legs, an inability to keep them still, and problems with her hands. She described dropping things without realizing it, referring to it as "incoordination."

Based on what I know now, these are textbook early signs of Huntington's. But the doctor's notes painted a different picture. He wrote: *"Patient has likely RLS (restless leg syndrome) based on her symptoms. Her physical examination also shows possible associated neuropathy. Will do an EMG. She is interested in being investigated for Huntington's given her family history. Will order genetic testing, but at this time, her exam and history are not really suggestive of this disease."* He also noted symptoms such as snoring, daytime sleepiness, and poor focus, and then referred her to a sleep clinic. He never ordered the genetic testing.

It's true that HD is rare, and sometimes even physicians miss it. But Mom was trying. She was reporting her symptoms, documenting what was happening, and even requesting to be tested for HD because there was a history of it in her family. It just wasn't enough.

Her persistence deserved more attention. And while I cannot change the past, I share this in the hope that others will listen closely to their loved ones and their own intuition, especially when something feels off. Early signs matter. Stories matter. And sometimes, patients know more than they're given credit for.

Tuesday, Oct. 16, 2018
AM   DR CUVA Apt — ME 2:15
Pain on top of pain —
has stopped But I have
problems with the following:
① Thinking I can more at
lightning speed
② I nattentive
③ feeling like my
head will explode if
I put one more new
thought there.

*Mom's notes as she was trying to grapple with all the symptoms
she was having*

excessive day time
sleepiness

Dementia

Alzheimer's

Menopaus

Narcolepsy
Social Media

More notes on symptoms and possible causes

When she wasn't documenting her symptoms, she was documenting how she felt and feeding herself hope. "I Brushed My Hair" is a beautiful piece pulling in her creative mind.

I Brushed My Hair

I brushed my hair
this morning.
Felt the winds gentle touch.
Listened to a bird talk.
Absorbed 10,000 shades
of orange. And red. And green.
And yellow. And bronze.
10,000 shades of brown
in the corn patch.

I brushed my hair
in the cool October morning
air, for the first time
in a long time.
Page One — DTG

I Brushed My Hair - Page 2

I hope I have many more days, to brush my hair and close my eyes and recall the love song I listened to last night. A sixteenth century ballad? I do believe the orater made that statement. I thought of the the timber of his voice and the smile that filled his face.

I brushed my hair this morning. Thank you, Lord, for this time and this place.

The End — DTZ 10/1/12

Just as her writing has helped me process my childhood, I think she was processing hers and finding gratitude amidst the trauma. She often wrote of how grateful she was for colors and for those around her, especially her grandchildren. And she prayed. She prayed for herself, for her children, and for her grandchildren. She prayed for our safety, and she prayed for the will to carry on.

Lord, I need help. You have brought me to this healing place, this healing space, and I pray You give me the courage to continue on.

I pray my grandchildren never have to fear if they hear feet coming that it is someone the love coming to harm them and they never have to fear going to school and like about the bruises and scrapes, they will never miss school because of choking bruises around their neck please, Lord. let them not know these pains. Let them know the joy of your love and the wonders you have for them, and keep them safe in your loving arms. Thank You, Dear Heavenly Father. In Jesus Name I Pray

Amen!

Huntington's disease was originally called Huntington's chorea. The word chorea originates from the Greek word choros, which means "to dance." Chorea is a symptom where your body involuntarily fidgets or jerks. It's a common symptom of HD. I find irony in this poem titled "Dance," talking about an arm that will not write. "Hold on tight." I don't know who Jacky is, but I love this one.

DANCE

A disgruntled arm
that will not write—
a drummer that looks
at life and screams,
"Hold on tight."
And Jacky.
Soft spoken Jacky.

We four remain.
To claim all
the fame?
From this we will
refrain.
Clementine.
Here we go again.

A walk in
the rain
is called for.
Dance.

Darlin

Dance

A disgruntled arm that will not write –

A drummer that looks at life and screams "hold on tight"

And Jacky.

Soft spoken Jacky.

We four remain.

To claim all the fame?

From this we will refrain.

Clementine.

Here we go again.

A walk in the rain is called for.

Dance.

DTG

When she was diagnosed, she was at the height of her suffering. The disease was progressing quickly. Still, the diagnosis gave us access to much-needed support. The Huntington's Disease Society of America (HDSA) was such a blessing to us. We immediately leaned in. They helped us get a social worker who worked with us 1:1 on next steps for Mom. They also helped my sister and me navigate the process to get ourselves tested for HD. They shared information on conferences we could attend. There were ample resources on everything from caregiving to advocacy to family issues, and I researched anything that I thought could be helpful. I joined the board of directors of the Tennessee Chapter and continue to be an advocate to this day.

HDSA Team Hope Walk after Mom was diagnosed.
Left to right: two friends with their son, Mom with her cane,
my husband Matt holding our daughter Opal, me holding
our daughter Eleanor, and two more friends. Front right holding
the balloon is our son, Townes. We were waiting to find out
if my sister and I carried the genetic mutation.

A BEAUTIFUL ENDING

Mom's health was already declining when the COVID-19 pandemic hit in 2020. Navigating care decisions for my mom was one of the hardest things I've ever done, and the pandemic flung us all into uncharted territory. We did the best we could with the information we had at the time. After consulting several members of her care team, we made the heartbreaking decision to take away her car because it was no longer safe for her to drive. She wasn't in possession of all of her faculties. It was the last piece of independence she had left, and taking it away sent her into a downward spiral.

Even before losing her car, Mom was struggling. She had trouble managing her medications, maintaining hygiene, making safe choices in her housing community, and eating well. Depression was already there, but once her autonomy was gone, it deepened. I started getting daily calls from her caregiver, sharing that Mom had no will to live. The light in her was dimming, and I didn't know what to do.

We had another round of discussions with her care team, and we moved her into an assisted living facility near my sister. My sister decided to be there to help facilitate one of Mom's telehealth appointments with her neurologist at Vanderbilt. It was during that visit, while checking her vitals, that they realized her oxygen was critically low. My sister rushed Mom to

Vanderbilt, where they were familiar with her history and care. We learned that only a portion of one of Mom's lungs was functioning.

The doctors gently urged us to begin thinking about palliative care, the goal being to keep Mom comfortable and provide relief from her symptoms for however long she continued to live with HD. My sister and I decided that she would spend the rest of her life surrounded by family.

Initially, we took turns caring for her, but my sister eventually became the primary caregiver. Her kids were older, and her work schedule allowed more flexibility. I helped in other ways, such as funding renovations to her home to create extra space and add a walk-in shower for Mom. It was hard on my nieces, but also meaningful. They learned a lot by having her close. It wasn't perfect, but it was real, and it was full of love.

As her illness progressed, her anger softened. I think she understood she was close to death and, of course, the medicine helped. Kindness rose to the surface, and that's how we were able to spend our final days with her.

But of course, Mom couldn't just quietly live out her days with Huntington's. While staying with my sister, she began experiencing vaginal bleeding. A trip to her oncologist in Nashville revealed that she was also battling ovarian cancer. The pain was worsening, and my sister felt it was time to move her to hospice so she could receive stronger medication. Mom was ready, but I wasn't.

She came to stay with me in Nashville, and I took a week off work just to be with her. I tried different things to ease her discomfort, including THC lotion and gummies from a local dispensary. She liked the gummies; they gave her relief without making her feel groggy.

That week was one of the best we ever had. We laughed. I read to her. She played her records and danced with her grandkids as best she could. On the day I was preparing to take her back home, I had been thinking about taking her to the Catholic church where I was baptized. In the car, just before we reached the turn, she looked over at me and said, "Would you like to take me to that Catholic church where you were baptized?" It was like she read my mind. I burst into tears. I called the church, and a priest met us in the parking lot to pray over her, since walking was difficult.

The universe connects mothers to their children in mysterious ways. Just as the placenta gives life, that connection never fades. At that moment, I knew she felt what I needed, and she gave it to me.

About a week later, I felt that same pull to see her again. Everyone at my sister's house was sick, but she assured me it was just a cold. It was 2020, and COVID-19 was running rampant. We went anyway. Within minutes, my husband turned to me and said, "I'm pretty sure everyone in this house has COVID." I panicked, and we ended up staying the night with my dad.

The next morning, we went back to say goodbye. I gave Mom a shower, brushed her hair, and we snuggled. She was tired, so we let her rest and headed back to Nashville.

As soon as we got home, I lay down in bed to take a nap, and my phone rang. It was my sister. Mom had fallen and couldn't get up. My sister had to call 911 for assistance in lifting Mom up from the floor. I left immediately and made it in time to sit with her and watch almost a full episode of *Schitt's Creek*. She sat beside me in a chair. That was the beginning of the end.

The next day was sweet and sacred. Family came to the house to see her. When she was awake, we sang to her, surrounded her with love, and held her hand. Her moments of wakefulness grew shorter, and we shifted to making her as comfortable as possible. Watching someone you love slip away is excruciating. There's no pain like it. But if she had to go, I'm grateful it was like this: surrounded by music, peace, and those who love her.

I told her I was sorry. For not knowing, for not treating her the way a person with a rare genetic disease should be treated, for not helping more. She forgave me. She told me she would always be my angel.

Plain daisies are really alright. Just not even a little uptight. Blowing in the wind showing the things they approve. Their kindness will really effect you.
-Darlene Gaynor (DTG)

A thank you I sent out after Mom's funeral. We received so many gifts and flowers that they filled an entire room. I wanted to thank everyone for the outpouring of love, so I mailed everyone copies of this note. The picture is of a double rainbow at my sister's house immediately following Mom's funeral. I pulled the poem from a post on Mom's Facebook page. I had all the kids sign the card on the inside.

Sometimes, life is really hard, and when it is, you have to be brave. Do the best you can. How you treat people truly matters. Put your faith in God. Take the good with the bad in people. Forgive, no matter what. Always be ready for an adventure with friends and family. Care for those who cannot care for themselves. Never judge because it's impossible to know what someone is going through. Words can hurt, so choose them wisely.

These are just a few of the things my mother taught me, and I never want to forget them. My mother was, and always will be, my angel. Life threw everything at her, and she fought hard. I loved her with all my heart when she was on this earth, and I will always love her.

I would be remiss not to mention her best friend, Stella, who stood by our side through everything. Mom wrote often about Stella and the circle of close friends who meant the world to her. When Mom took her final breath, Stella was there. Truth be told, she even sent us to bed when the time came. We'd been awake for over 24 hours and had already called hospice, but Stella stayed. She wouldn't leave her. That kind of loyalty is rare.

There was one surreal moment I'll never forget. I did a soft yoga "*om,*" just trying to bring peace into the room. After she had been still for quite some time, Mom suddenly opened her eyes wide. Energy is real. I've seen a lot of strange things in life, but that was the most inexplicable, the most profound.

After the funeral, we gathered at my sister's house for a meal with family members. I couldn't believe it when I saw the double rainbow, which felt like a sign of hope from Mom, telling us to carry on and that she'll always be with us. Later on, while driving to my dad's house to pick up my nieces, I saw the most beautiful flowers I'd ever seen. They were wildflowers, and they looked like a beautiful bouquet that Mom had put together just for me. The wind moved through them differently, like a whisper, a sign. These wild, seemingly random bits of nature felt perfectly arranged for me to see. A quiet reminder that though Mom is physically gone, she will always be with us.

Mom faced her illness with the quiet strength of a wildflower. She didn't resist it. She accepted her fate, yet still found ways to thrive. Like a seed carried by the wind, she took root wherever life placed her, blossoming effortlessly. She became a living testament to resilience, to quiet growth, and to the enduring beauty that can bloom even in the harshest conditions.

INSPIRED CLOSE

Writing this book was more than therapeutic; it was transformative. I got lost in all the creative ways my mom channeled her energy, and in doing so, I found pieces of her I had long forgotten. I'm incredibly grateful that she wrote, that she documented her world, and that she fought so hard for joy in the face of so much unknown.

As I researched Huntington's disease, I came across story after story of suffering. But I also found glimmers of resilience. Caregivers writing cards for their HD patients. Online support groups, where people share encouraging messages for others struggling to care for their loved ones. Patients who found small ways to cope, such as eating more calories to manage their symptoms. I wondered if this was also true for my mother. I wondered what kept her resilient Her writings, I think, for sure. What else? I don't know. I will never know exactly what worked, but I do know this: She always tried her best.

That spirit is what I hope stays with you. I hope this book reminds you that what appears on the surface is rarely the whole story. In every great leadership class I've ever taken, we talk about the iceberg model and how most of what shapes a person lies beneath the waterline, invisible to others. This book is no exception. It's my attempt to show the deeper layers, the quiet courage, the unseen grace.

We are all carrying more than we show. But the world can be softer, kinder, and more beautiful when we choose to look deeper and when we choose to remain hopeful. If this book has done anything, I hope it has helped you see the flowers in a different light. One where, maybe for the first time, they are all your favorite.

RESOURCES

The Huntington's Disease Society of America (HDSA) is the premier nonprofit organization dedicated to improving the lives of everyone affected by Huntington's disease. From community services and education to advocacy and research, HDSA is the world's leader in providing help for today, hope for tomorrow for people with Huntington's disease and their families. In the battle against Huntington's disease no one fights alone. *At HDSA — family is everything!* For more information, visit **hdsa.org**

The Huntington's Disease Program at Vanderbilt University Medical Center focuses exclusively on diagnosing and caring for individuals with this genetic, neurodegenerative disorder as well as providing support for their families. Here, you'll find a care team that's committed to delivering expert and compassionate care, which you'll experience throughout your treatment journey with us. For more information, visit **vanderbilthealth.com/program/huntingtons-disease**

The Other Dr. Gilmer **by Benjamin Gilmer** explores the true story of a doctor who takes over a rural North Carolina clinic and discovers that his predecessor—also named Dr. Gilmer—is imprisoned for murdering his father. Unraveling the mystery, the book examines the intersections of mental illness, justice, and compassion in the U.S. healthcare and criminal systems. For more information, visit **benjamingilmer.com**

***Livable Lives: Conversations with the Huntington's Disease Community* by Dr. Christy Dearien** was recommended to me by Dr. Claassen at Vanderbilt. This book would have been immensely valuable in the early stages of finding out about Mom having HD, and I would recommend it to people wanting to learn more about how to live with HD. For more information, visit **christydearien.com/book**

Al-Anon Family Groups is a mutual support program for people whose lives have been affected by someone else's drinking. By sharing common experiences and applying the Al-Anon principles, families and friends of alcoholics can bring positive changes to their individual situations, whether or not the alcoholic admits the existence of a drinking problem or seeks help. For more information, visit **al-anon.org**

ACKNOWLEDGMENTS

To my husband, Matt, for being the most amazing partner and father. Our life together is sweeter than I could have ever imagined.

To Eleanor, Opal, and Townes for bringing me great joy and always keeping me on my toes. You didn't get to spend much time with your grandmother, and I hope this book gives you an understanding of how amazing she was.

To my sister, Ruby, for being by my side from the beginning. You stepped in with our mom when I couldn't. I appreciate your grit. Thanks for being one of the first readers of this book.

To Ady, Aly, and Ayva for making me Aunt Birdie. You are all so smart and strong. Watching you grow up has been a great gift. I hope you enjoy the book.

To my cousins for all of the group chats, cut flowers, four-wheeler rides, and life celebrations. We learned to run through the mud together and get up when we fell down. Thanks for always showing up.

To all of my mom's friends, especially Gail Reed, Stella Roma, and Donna Keck: You have shown me how meaning-ful true friendship really is. You are angels.

To my previous colleagues at Cisco and in the industry solutions group, for all of your support and love during my mom's diagnosis, awaiting my DNA results, and the two years of caregiving and bereavement after she passed. Especially Heather Parkison for the long phone calls.

To my mentors and sponsors, Lynn Winans, Carol Stroud, Todd Gurela, and Troy Yoder (and Vivian Warner and Anna Belle O'Brien, who are no longer with us), for all of your guidance. I wouldn't be where I am today without you.

To my dad's sisters, Wilma, Mary, Ruth, Paula, and Bernadette: Thank you for believing in me and helping with buying shoes and school supplies, inspiring me, sponsoring academic and sporting events, pushing me to run marathons, and enabling me to live my dreams.

To my best friend, Jill, for always always having my back.

To Emily and Tommy for being the first in the HMS tribe that turned non-HMS tribe. I'm incredibly grateful you are all a part of my life, including Drew, Shawnte, Chemeka, Reena, and Liz. You all mean the world to me.

To my long-distance Vanderbilt crew, Nate Gonzalez, Dr. Elizabeth Copenhaver, and Kelly Walsh, for knowing when to check in and exactly what to say.

To the Johnson family for sharing all the important life moments since the Roberts family was established. We wouldn't want to do it without you.

To Debbie, Monica, Jesse, and Josie for making me a part of the family. Sometimes things are hard for me, and I'm not always the easiest to get along with, but I love you guys and am happy to be a part of the family.

To Josh and Allison for supporting us and attending all of the HD events. I especially love how giving Matt and Josh are when it's time for the bourbon tasting events.

To Donnie and Mary Umphrey, for singing and praying and being there on the hardest day of my life.

To Dr. Claassen, for writing the foreword to this book, and for all you do for the HD community.

To my editor and friend, Clare, who was there when I first decided to write this book. Your attention to detail is beyond what I could've done alone. Thanks for pushing me to be vulnerable and inspiring me to cross the finish line.

To Shanda and the team at Transcendent Publishing, for helping to make it a reality that my mother could become a published author. This book turned out beautifully thanks to your thoughtful work.

To my dad, for teaching me how to be independent and strong.

To my mom, for always being there to the best of your capabilities. You're a published author now!

ABOUT THE AUTHOR

Audrey Roberts is a leader in sustainability innovation and technology, helping organizations navigate modernization, transformation, and systems-level change. She graduated from Vanderbilt University, where she studied Economics and German and expanded her worldview through study abroad programs in Germany, Austria, and Guatemala.

Over the course of her career, she has led major transformation initiatives across Fortune 100 companies, shaping strategies, launching sustainable technology solutions, and helping health systems respond to urgent challenges, including the COVID-19 pandemic. In 2023, she returned to university to pursue an MBA and an M.S. in Sustainability, driven by her passion for the intersection of health, equity, and the environment.

Audrey lives in Nashville, TN, where she and her husband Matt are raising three children in a life filled with carpool lanes, constant questions, and big hearts. This is her first book.